TECHNICAL, BUSINESS, AND **LEGAL DIMENSIONS** OF **PROTECTING CHILDREN** FROM **PORNOGRAPHY** ON THE **INTERNET**

PROCEEDINGS OF A WORKSHOP

Committee to Study Tools and Strategies for
Protecting Kids from Pornography and Their Applicability to
Other Inappropriate Internet Content

Computer Science and Telecommunications Board
Division on Engineering and Physical Sciences
National Research Council

Board on Children, Youth, and Families
Division of Behavioral and Social Sciences and Education
National Research Council and Institute of Medicine

NATIONAL ACADEMY PRESS
Washington, D.C.

NATIONAL ACADEMY PRESS • 2101 Constitution Avenue, N.W. • Washington, DC 20418

NOTICE: The project that is the subject of this report was approved by the Governing Board of the National Research Council, whose members are drawn from the councils of the National Academy of Sciences, the National Academy of Engineering, and the Institute of Medicine. The members of the committee responsible for the report were chosen for their special competences and with regard for appropriate balance.

The study of which this workshop report was a part was supported by Grant No. 1999-JN-FX-0071 between the National Academy of Sciences and the U.S. Departments of Justice and Education; Grant No. P0073380 between the National Academy of Sciences and the W.K. Kellogg Foundation; awards (unnumbered) from the Microsoft Corporation and IBM; and National Research Council funds. Any opinions, findings, conclusions, or recommendations expressed in this publication are those of the author(s) and do not necessarily reflect the views of the organizations or agencies that provided support for this project. Any opinions, findings, conclusions, or recommendations expressed in this material are those of the symposium presenters and do not necessarily reflect the views of the sponsors.

International Standard Book Number 0-309-08326-5

Additional copies of this report are available from:

National Academy Press
2101 Constitution Avenue, N.W.
Box 285
Washington, DC 20055
800/624-6242
202/334-3313 (in the Washington metropolitan area)

Copyright 2002 by the National Academy of Sciences. All rights reserved.

Printed in the United States of America

THE NATIONAL ACADEMIES

National Academy of Sciences
National Academy of Engineering
Institute of Medicine
National Research Council

The **National Academy of Sciences** is a private, nonprofit, self-perpetuating society of distinguished scholars engaged in scientific and engineering research, dedicated to the furtherance of science and technology and to their use for the general welfare. Upon the authority of the charter granted to it by the Congress in 1863, the Academy has a mandate that requires it to advise the federal government on scientific and technical matters. Dr. Bruce M. Alberts is president of the National Academy of Sciences.

The **National Academy of Engineering** was established in 1964, under the charter of the National Academy of Sciences, as a parallel organization of outstanding engineers. It is autonomous in its administration and in the selection of its members, sharing with the National Academy of Sciences the responsibility for advising the federal government. The National Academy of Engineering also sponsors engineering programs aimed at meeting national needs, encourages education and research, and recognizes the superior achievements of engineers. Dr. Wm. A. Wulf is president of the National Academy of Engineering.

The **Institute of Medicine** was established in 1970 by the National Academy of Sciences to secure the services of eminent members of appropriate professions in the examination of policy matters pertaining to the health of the public. The Institute acts under the responsibility given to the National Academy of Sciences by its congressional charter to be an adviser to the federal government and, upon its own initiative, to identify issues of medical care, research, and education. Dr. Kenneth I. Shine is president of the Institute of Medicine.

The **National Research Council** was organized by the National Academy of Sciences in 1916 to associate the broad community of science and technology with the Academy's purposes of furthering knowledge and advising the federal government. Functioning in accordance with general policies determined by the Academy, the Council has become the principal operating agency of both the National Academy of Sciences and the National Academy of Engineering in providing services to the government, the public, and the scientific and engineering communities. The Council is administered jointly by both Academies and the Institute of Medicine. Dr. Bruce M. Alberts and Dr. Wm. A. Wulf are chairman and vice chairman, respectively, of the National Research Council.

COMMITTEE TO STUDY TOOLS AND STRATEGIES FOR PROTECTING KIDS FROM PORNOGRAPHY AND THEIR APPLICABILITY TO OTHER INAPPROPRIATE INTERNET CONTENT

RICHARD THORNBURGH, Kirkpatrick & Lockhart LLP, *Chair*
NICHOLAS J. BELKIN, Rutgers University
WILLIAM J. BYRON, Holy Trinity Parish
SANDRA L. CALVERT, Georgetown University
DAVID FORSYTH, University of California at Berkeley
DANIEL GEER, @Stake
LINDA HODGE, Parent Teacher Association
MARILYN GELL MASON, Independent Consultant
MILO MEDIN, Excite@Home
JOHN B. RABUN, National Center for Missing and Exploited Children
ROBIN RASKIN, *FamilyPC* Magazine
ROBERT SCHLOSS, IBM T.J. Watson Research Center
JANET WARD SCHOFIELD, University of Pittsburgh
GEOFFREY R. STONE, University of Chicago
WINIFRED B. WECHSLER, Independent Consultant

Staff

HERBERT S. LIN, Senior Scientist and Study Director
GAIL PRITCHARD, Program Officer (through June 2001)
LAURA OST, Consultant
JOAH G. IANOTTA, Research Assistant
JANICE SABUDA, Senior Project Assistant
DANIEL D. LLATA, Senior Project Assistant (through May 2001)

COMPUTER SCIENCE AND TELECOMMUNICATIONS BOARD

DAVID D. CLARK, Massachusetts Institute of Technology, *Chair*
DAVID BORTH, Motorola Labs
JAMES CHIDDIX, AOL Time Warner
JOHN M. CIOFFI, Stanford University
ELAINE COHEN, University of Utah
W. BRUCE CROFT, University of Massachusetts at Amherst
THOMAS E. DARCIE, AT&T Labs Research
JOSEPH FARRELL, University of California at Berkeley
JEFFREY M. JAFFE, Bell Laboratories, Lucent Technologies
ANNA KARLIN, University of Washington
BUTLER W. LAMPSON, Microsoft Corporation
EDWARD D. LAZOWSKA, University of Washington
DAVID LIDDLE, U.S. Venture Partners
TOM M. MITCHELL, Carnegie Mellon University
DONALD NORMAN, Nielsen Norman Group
DAVID A. PATTERSON, University of California at Berkeley
HENRY (HANK) PERRITT, Illinois Institute of Technology
BURTON SMITH, Cray Inc.
TERRY SMITH, University of California at Santa Barbara
LEE SPROULL, New York University
JEANNETTE M. WING, Carnegie Mellon University

Staff

MARJORY S. BLUMENTHAL, Director
HERBERT S. LIN, Senior Scientist
ALAN S. INOUYE, Senior Program Officer
JON EISENBERG, Senior Program Officer
LYNETTE I. MILLETT, Program Officer
CYNTHIA PATTERSON, Program Officer
STEVEN WOO, Program Officer
JANET BRISCOE, Administrative Officer
DAVID PADGHAM, Research Associate
MARGARET HUYNH, Senior Project Assistant
DAVID DRAKE, Senior Project Assistant
JANICE SABUDA, Senior Project Assistant
JENNIFER BISHOP, Senior Project Assistant
BRANDYE WILLIAMS, Staff Assistant

BOARD ON CHILDREN, YOUTH, AND FAMILIES

EVAN CHARNEY, University of Massachusetts Medical School, *Chair*
JAMES A. BANKS, University of Washington
DONALD COHEN, Yale University
THOMAS DEWITT, Children's Hospital Medical Center of Cincinnati
MARY JANE ENGLAND, Washington Business Group on Health
MINDY FULLILOVE, Columbia University
PATRICIA GREENFIELD, University of California at Los Angeles
RUTH T. GROSS, Stanford University
KEVIN GRUMBACH, University of California at San Francisco, San Francisco General Hospital
NEAL HALFON, University of California at Los Angeles School of Public Health
MAXINE HAYES, Washington State Department of Health
MARGARET HEAGARTY, Columbia University
RENÉE R. JENKINS, Howard University
HARRIET KITZMAN, University of Rochester
SANDERS KORENMAN, Baruch College, City University of New York
HON. CINDY LEDERMAN, Juvenile Justice Center, Dade County, Florida
VONNIE McLOYD, University of Michigan
GARY SANDEFUR, University of Wisconsin-Madison
ELIZABETH SPELKE, Massachusetts Institute of Technology
RUTH STEIN, Montefiore Medical Center

Liaisons

ELEANOR E. MACCOBY (Liaison, Division of Behavioral and Social Sciences and Education), Department of Psychology (emeritus), Stanford University
WILLIAM ROPER (Liaison, IOM Council), Institute of Medicine, University of North Carolina, Chapel Hill

Staff

MICHELE D. KIPKE, Director (through September 2001)
MARY GRAHAM, Associate Director, Dissemination and Communications
SONJA WOLFE, Administrative Associate
ELENA NIGHTINGALE, Scholar-in-Residence
JOAH G. IANNOTTA, Research Assistant

Preface

In response to a mandate from Congress in conjunction with the Protection of Children from Sexual Predators Act of 1998, the Computer Science and Telecommunications Board (CSTB) and the Board on Children, Youth, and Families of the National Research Council (NRC) and the Institute of Medicine established the Committee to Study Tools and Strategies for Protecting Kids from Pornography and Their Applicability to Other Inappropriate Internet Content.

To collect input and to disseminate useful information to the nation on this question, the committee held two public workshops. On December 13, 2000, in Washington, D.C., the committee convened a workshop to focus on nontechnical strategies that could be effective in a broad range of settings (e.g., home, school, libraries) in which young people might be online. This workshop brought together researchers, educators, policy makers, and other key stakeholders to consider and discuss these approaches and to identify some of the benefits and limitations of various nontechnical strategies. The December workshop is summarized in *Nontechnical Strategies to Reduce Children's Exposure to Inappropriate Material on the Internet: Summary of a Workshop*.[1]

---

[1] National Research Council and Institute of Medicine, *Nontechnical Strategies to Reduce Children's Exposure to Inappropriate Material on the Internet: Summary of a Workshop*, Computer Science and Telecommunications Board and Board on Children, Youth, and Families, Joah G. Iannotta, ed., Washington, D.C.: National Academy Press, 2001.

The second workshop was held on March 7, 2001, in Redwood City, California. This second workshop focused on some of the technical, business, and legal factors that affect how one might choose to protect kids from pornography on the Internet. The present report provides, in the form of edited transcripts, the presentations at that workshop. Obviously, because the report reflects the presentations on that day, it is not intended to be a comprehensive review of all of the technical, business, and legal issues that might be relevant to this subject. All views expressed in this report are those of the speaker (who sometimes is a member of the study committee speaking for himself or herself). Most importantly, this report should not be construed as representing the views of the Committee to Study Tools and Strategies for Protecting Kids from Pornography and Their Applicability to Other Inappropriate Internet Content; the Computer Science and Telecommunications Board; the Board on Children, Youth, and Families; the National Research Council; or the Institute of Medicine.

The report contains 17 chapters, each of which is essentially an edited transcript of the various briefings to the committee during the workshop. Questions and comments from the audience and committee members are included as footnotes. The first four chapters are devoted to the basics of information retrieval and searching. The next three (Chapters 5-7) address some of the technology and business dimensions of filtering, the process through which certain types of putatively objectionable content are blocked from display on a user's screen. Two chapters (Chapters 8-9) then address technical and infrastructural dimensions of authentication—the process of proving that one is who one asserts to be. The next three chapters (Chapters 10-12) address automated approaches to negotiating individualized policy preferences and dealing with issues of intellectual property (and preventing unauthorized parties from viewing protected material). Chapter 13 addresses the problems associated with a dot-xxx domain for "cordoning off" sexually explicit material on the Internet. Chapters 14-16 cover various issues associated with business models for the Internet, and the final chapter, Chapter 17, discusses one legal scholar's perspective on regulating sexually explicit material on the Internet.

Gail Pritchard was largely responsible for assembling the speakers at this workshop, and Laura Ost generated the first draft of the report.

This report was reviewed in draft form by individuals chosen for their diverse perspectives and technical expertise, in accordance with procedures approved by the NRC's Report Review Committee. The purpose of this independent review is to provide candid and critical comments that will assist the institution in making the published report as sound as possible and to ensure that the report meets institutional standards for objectivity, evidence, and responsiveness to the study charge. The review comments and draft manuscript remain confidential to protect the integrity of the deliberative process.

We thank the following individuals for their participation in the review of these workshop proceedings:

William Aspray, Computing Research Association,
Hinrich Schütze, Novation Biosciences, and
Frederick Weingarten, American Library Association.

Although these individuals reviewed the report, they were not asked to endorse it, nor did they see the final draft of the report before its release. The review of this report was overseen by Peter Blair of the Division on Engineering and Physical Sciences. Appointed by the National Research Council, he was responsible for making certain that an independent examination of this report was carried out in accordance with institutional procedures and that all review comments were carefully considered. Responsibility for the final content of this report rests entirely with the authoring committee and the institution.

Herbert S. Lin, Senior Scientist and Study Director
Computer Science and Telecommunications Board

Contents

1 BASIC CONCEPTS IN INFORMATION RETRIEVAL　　　　1
　　Nicholas Belkin
　1.1　Definitions and System Design, 1
　1.2　Problems, 2

2　TEXT CATEGORIZATION AND ANALYSIS　　　　5
　　David Lewis and Hinrich Schütze
　2.1　Text Categorization, 5
　2.2　Advanced Text Technology, 7

3　CATEGORIZATION OF IMAGES　　　　11
　　David Forsyth
　3.1　Challenges in Object Recognition, 11
　3.2　Screening of Pornographic Images, 12
　3.3　The Future, 14

4　THE TECHNOLOGY OF SEARCH ENGINES　　　　16
　　Ray Larson
　4.1　Overview, 16
　4.2　Boolean Search Logic, 17
　4.3　The Vector Space Model, 18
　4.4　Searching the World Wide Web, 19

5	CYBER PATROL: A MAJOR FILTERING PRODUCT *Susan Getgood* 5.1 Introduction, 23 5.2 Why Filter?, 24 5.3 SuperScout and Cyber Patrol, 25 5.4 The Review Process, 29 5.5 The Future, 31	23
6	ADVANCED TECHNIQUES FOR AUTOMATIC WEB FILTERING *Michel Bilello* 6.1 Background, 33 6.2 The WIPE System, 34	33
7	A CRITIQUE OF FILTERING *Bennett Haselton* 7.1 Introduction, 36 7.2 Deficiencies in Filtering Programs, 37 7.3 Experiments by Peacefire.org, 38 7.4 Circumvention of Blocking Software, 45	36
8	AUTHENTICATION TECHNOLOGIES *Eddie Zeitler* 8.1 The Process of Identification, 48 8.2 Challenges and Solutions, 50	48
9	INFRASTRUCTURE FOR AGE VERIFICATION *Fred Cotton* 9.1 The Real World Versus the Internet, 53 9.2 Solutions, 56 9.3 The Extent of the Problem, 59	53
10	AUTOMATED POLICY PREFERENCE NEGOTIATION *Deirdre Mulligan*	62
11	DIGITAL RIGHTS MANAGEMENT TECHNOLOGY *John Blumenthal* 11.1 Technology and Policy Constraints, 65 11.2 Designing a Solution to Fit the Constraints, 67 11.3 Protecting Children, 73 11.4 Summary, 75	65

12	A TRUSTED THIRD PARTY IN DIGITAL RIGHTS MANAGEMENT *David Maher* 12.1 InterTrust Technologies, 77 12.2 Countermeasures and Hackers, 80 12.3 Summary, 84	76
13	PROBLEMS WITH A DOT-XXX DOMAIN *Donald Eastlake*	85
14	BUSINESS DIMENSIONS: THE EDUCATION MARKET *Irv Shapiro* 14.1 The Role of Teachers, 90 14.2 Historical Perspective, 91 14.3 The School Marketplace, 92	90
15	BUSINESS MODELS: KID-FRIENDLY INTERNET BUSINESSES *Brian Pass* 15.1 Building an Internet Business, 96 15.2 Comparing Business Models, 98 15.3 The Role of Parents, 103	96
16	BUSINESS MODELS BASED ON ADVERTISING *Chris Kelly* 16.1 Comparison of Advertising Models, 104 16.2 Portals, Advertising Networks, and Targeting, 105 16.3 Choice of Models, 106 16.4 Advertising, Regulation, and Kids, 107	104
17	CONSTITUTIONAL LAW AND THE LAW OF CYBERSPACE *Larry Lessig* 17.1 Introduction, 110 17.2 Regulation in Cyberspace, 111 17.3 Possible Solutions, 112 17.4 Practical Considerations, 118	110
APPENDIX: BIOGRAPHIES OF PRESENTERS		124

1

Basic Concepts in Information Retrieval

Nicholas Belkin

1.1 DEFINITIONS AND SYSTEM DESIGN

Information retrieval and information filtering are different functions. Information retrieval is intended to support people who are actively seeking or searching for information, as in Internet searching. Information retrieval typically assumes a static or relatively static database against which people search. Search engine companies construct these databases by sending out "spiders" and then indexing the Web pages they find. By contrast, information filtering supports people in the passive monitoring for desired information. It is typically understood to be concerned with an active incoming stream of information objects.

The problem in information retrieval and information filtering is that decisions must be made for every document or information object regarding whether or not to show it to the person who is retrieving the information. Initially, a profile describing the user's information needs is set up to facilitate such decision making; this profile may be modified over the long term through the use of user models. These models are based on a person's behavior—decisions, reading behaviors, and so on, which may change the original profile. Both information retrieval and information filtering attempt to maximize the good material that a person sees (that which is likely to be appropriate to the information problem at hand) and minimize the bad material.

When people refer to filtering, they often really mean information retrieval. That is, they are not concerned with dynamic streams of documents but rather with databases that are already constructed and in which there is some way to represent the information objects and relate them to one another. Thus, filtering corresponds to the Boolean filter in information retrieval: a yes/no decision.

Most search engines designed for the World Wide Web use the principle of "best match," that is, not making yes/no decisions but, rather, ranking information objects with respect to some representation of the information problem. Thus, the basic processes in information retrieval or information filtering are the representations of information objects and of information needs, or more generally, the problem or goal that the person has in mind. The retrieval techniques themselves then compare needs with objects.

The interaction of the user with other components of the system is important. In fact, the prevailing view in information retrieval research is that the most effective approach for helping a user obtain the appropriate information is relevance feedback, in which the system takes into account whether a person likes or dislikes a document as it automatically re-represents the user's query. This leads to performance improvements of as much as 150 percent—much better than any other technique. Thus, the person's judgment of the information objects is an important part of the process. The user is an actor in the information retrieval system, because many of the processes depend on his or her expression and interpretation of the need. The relevance of a document cannot be determined unless the person is considered a part of the system.

The second important part of the system is the information resource, a collection of information objects that has been selected, organized, and represented according to some schema. The third component is the intermediary—a device or person that mediates between the information resource and the user and that has knowledge of the user, the user's problem, and the types of users that exist, as well as the information resource, the way the resource is organized, what it contains, and so on. The intermediary supports the interaction between people and the information objects and knowledge resource, through prediction and other means.

1.2 PROBLEMS

The representation of information problems is inherently uncertain, because people look for that which they do not know, and it is probably inappropriate to ask them to specify what they do not know. The representation of information objects requires interpretations by a human indexer, machine algorithm, or other entity. The problem is that anyone's interpretation of a particular text is likely to be different from anyone else's, and even different for the same person at different times. As our state of knowledge or problems change, our understanding of a text changes. Everyone has experienced the situation of finding a document not relevant at some point but highly relevant later on, perhaps for a different problem or perhaps because we, ourselves, are different. The easiest and most effective way to deal with this problem is to support users' interactions with information objects and let them take control.

Because of these uncertainties, the comparison of needs and information objects, or retrieval process, is also inherently uncertain and probabilistic. The understanding of information objects is subjective, and, therefore, representation is necessarily inconsistent. We do not know how well we are representing either the person's need or the information object. An extensive literature on interindexer consistency shows that when people are asked to represent an information object, even if they are highly trained in using the same meta-language (indexing language), they might achieve as much as only 60 to 70 percent consistency in tasks such as assigning descriptors. We will never achieve "ideal" information retrieval—that is, all the relevant documents and only the relevant documents, or precisely that one thing that a person wants.

The implication is that we must think of probabilistic ways of representing information problems. Even if computers were as smart as people, they probably could not do the job. A standard information retrieval result is that automatic indexing—in which algorithms do statistical word counting and indexing—leads to performance that is no worse, and often better, than systems in which people do manual indexing.

There is no reason to suppose that people will do a better job than machines, and neither one will do a perfect job, ever. Making absolute predictions in an inherently probabilistic environment is not a good idea.

Algorithms for representing information objects, or information problems, do give consistent representations. But they give one interpretation of the text, out of a great variety of possible representations, depending on the interpreter. Language is ambiguous in many ways: polysemy, synonymity, and so on. For example, a bank can be either a financial institution or something on the side of a river (polysemy). The context matters a lot in the interpretation.

The meta-language used to describe information objects, or linguistic objects, often is construed to be exactly the same as the textual language itself. But they are not the same. The similarity of the two languages has led to some confusion. In information retrieval, it has led to the idea that the words in the text represent the important concepts and, therefore, can be used to represent what the text is about. The confusion extends to image retrieval, because images can be ambiguous in at least as many ways as can language. Furthermore, there is no universal meta-language for describing images. People who are interested in images for advertising purposes have different ways to talk and think about them than do art historians, even though they may be searching for the same images. The lack of a common meta-language for images means that we need to think of special terms for images in special circumstances.

In attempting to prevent children from getting harmful material, it is possible to make approximations and give helpful direction. But in the end, that is the most that we can hope for. It is not a question of preventing someone from getting inappropriate material but, rather, of supporting the person in not getting it. At least part of the public policy concern is kids who are actively trying to get pornography, and it is unreasonable to suppose that information retrieval techniques will be useful in achieving the goal of preventing them from doing so.

There are a variety of users. The user might be a concerned parent or manager who suspects that something bad is going on. But mistakes are inevitable, and we need to figure out some way to deal with that. It is difficult to tell what anything means, and usually we get it wrong. Generally we want to design the tools so that getting it wrong is not as much of a nuisance as it otherwise might be.

2

Text Categorization and Analysis

David Lewis and Hinrich Schütze

2.1 TEXT CATEGORIZATION

Automatic text categorization is the primary language retrieval technology in content filtering for children. Text categorization is the sorting of text into groups, such as pornography, hate speech, violence, and unobjectionable content. A text categorizer looks at a Web page and decides into which of these groups a piece of text should fall. Applications of text categorization include filtering of e-mail, chat, or Web access; text indexing; and data mining.

Why is content filtering a categorization task? One way to frame the problem is to say that the categories are actions, such as "allow," "allow but warn," or "block." We either want to allow access to a Web page, allow access but also give a warning, or block access. Another way to frame the problem is to say that the categories are different types of content, such as news, sex education, pornography, or home pages. Depending on which category we put the page in, we will take different actions. For example, we want to block pornography and give access to news.

The automation of text categorization requires some input from people. The idea is to mimic what people do. Two parts of the task need to be automated. One is the categorization decision itself. The categorization decision says, for example, what we should do with a Web page. The second part to be automated is rule creation. We want to determine automatically the rules to apply.

Automation of the categorization decision requires a piece of software that applies rules to text. This is the best architecture because then we can change the behavior by changing the rules rather than rewriting the software every time. This automatic categorizer applies two types of rules. One type is extensional rules that explicitly list all sites that cannot be accessed (i.e., "blacklisted" sites) or, alternatively, all sites that can be accessed (e.g., kid-safe zones or "whitelisted" sites). The second type, which is technically more complicated, is intentional rules or keyword blocking. We look at the content of the page, and, if certain words occur, then we take certain actions, such as blocking access to that page. It can be more complicated than just a single word. For example, it can be logic based, where we use AND and OR operators, or it can be a weighted combination of different types of words.

Automated rule writing is called supervised learning. One or more persons are needed to provide samples of the types of decisions we wish to make. For example, we could ask a librarian to identify which of 500 texts or Web pages are pornography and which ones are not. This provides a training set of 500 sample decisions to be mimicked. The rule-writing software attempts to produce rules that mimic those categorization decisions. The goal is to mimic the categorization decisions made by people. The selection of the persons who provide the samples is fundamental, because whatever they do becomes the gold standard, which the machine tries to mimic. Everything depends on the particular persons and their judgments.

Research shows that supervised learning is at least as good as expert human rule writing. (Supervised learning is also very flexible. For example, foreign content is not a problem, as long as the content involves text rather than images.) The effectiveness of these methods is far from perfect—there is always some error rate—but sometimes it is near agreement with human performance levels. Still, the results differ from category to category, and it is not clear how directly it applies to, for example, pornography. As discussed in the next presentation, there is an inevitable trade-off between false positives and false negatives, and categories vary widely in difficulty. Substantially improved methods are not expected in the next 10 to 20 years.

It is not clear which text categorization techniques are most effective. Some recently developed techniques are not yet used commercially, so there may be incremental improvements. Nor is it clear how effective semiautomated categorization is, or whether the categories that are difficult for automated methods are the same as those that perplex people. With regard to spam e-mail, it is possible to circumvent it, but there is no foolproof way to filter it. The question is whether the error rate is acceptable.

This all comes back to community standards. We can train the classifier to predict the probability that a person would find an item inappropriate, and training can give equal weight to any number of community volunteers. In other words, we can build a machine that mimics a community standard. We take some people out of the community, get their judgments about what they find objectionable or not, and then build a machine that creates rules that mimic that behavior. But this does not solve the political question of how to define the community, who to select as representatives of that community, and where in that community to apply the filter. The technological capability does not solve the application issues in practice.

2.2 ADVANCED TEXT TECHNOLOGY

True text understanding will not happen for at least 20 or 30 years, and maybe never. Therein lies the problem, because to filter content with absolute accuracy we would need text understanding. As a result, there will always be an error rate; the question is how high it is.

The text categorization methods discussed above use the "bag-of-words" model. This is a simplistic machine representation of text. It takes all the words on a page and treats them as an unstructured list. If the text is "Dick Armey chooses Bob Shaffer to lead committee," then a representative list would be: Armey, Bob, chooses, committee, Dick, lead, Shaffer. The structure and context of the text is completely lost. This impoverished representation is the basis of text classification methods in existing content filters.

There are problems with this type of representation. It fails, in many cases, because of ambiguous words. The context is important. Ambiguous words such as "beaver" have both a hunter's meaning and a graphic meaning. Using the bag-of-words model alone, you cannot tell which meaning is relevant. The bag-of-words model is inherently problematic for these types of ambiguous words. Other words, such as "breast" and "blow," are not ambiguous but can be used pornographically. Again, if we use a bag-of-words model, then we lose context and cannot deal with these words properly. When context counts, the bag-of-words model fails.

The problem cannot be resolved fully by looking for adjacent words, as search engines do when they give higher weight to information objects that match the query and have certain words in the same sentence. There is a distinction between search engines and classification. Search engines compute a ranking of pages. The end users look at the top 10 or maybe the top 100 ranked pages. Because they are looking only at pages in which the signal is strongest and because they are making a relative judgment, this type of methodology works very well; the highest-rated pages are probably very relevant to the query.[1] But in classification, we have to make a decision about one page by itself. This is a much more difficult problem. By looking at the words that lie nearby, we cannot always make a decent statistical guess as to whether a situation is innocuous or not.

When context is important, when the bag-of-words model fails, pornography filters and content filters make errors. However—surprisingly—the bag-of-words model is effective in many applications, so it is not a hopeless basis for pornography filters despite its error rate. It always comes down to what error rate is acceptable.[2] To go beyond the bag-of-words model, a number of technologies are currently available: morphological analysis, part-of-speech tagging, translation, disambiguation, genre analysis, information extraction, syntactic analysis, and parsing. Even using these technologies, thorough text understanding will remain in the distant future; a 100-percent-accurate categorization decision cannot be made today. But these advanced text technologies can increase the accuracy of content filters, and this increased accuracy may be significant in some areas.

The first area relates to over-broad filters that block material that should not be blocked, raising free speech issues. It is relatively easy to build an over-broad filter, which blocks pornography very well but also blocks a lot of good content, like Dick Armey's home page. These over-broad filters may suffice in many circumstances. For example, there may be parents who would say, "As long as not a single pornographic page comes through, or it almost never happens, it is OK if my child cannot see a lot of good content." But these over-broad filters are problematic in many other settings, such as in libraries, where there is an issue of free speech. If a lot of good content is blocked, then that is problematic. Advanced technology can really make a difference, because by increasing the accuracy of the filter, less good content would be blocked.

---

[1]Milo Medin said that various search engine companies have come with a number of techniques to filter adult content, so that you have to turn on the capability to see certain types of references. Most of it is ranking based, but there are some other obvious things as well. Part of the challenge is that many adult sites are trying to get people to visit, so they fill their headers with all kinds of information that make it obvious what is going on. The question is, how practical is that?

[2]Milo Medin said that the people who run search engines have an economic interest in making their results as accurate as possible, to satisfy their subscribers. Normal large search engines want the adult-content filter to be as accurate as possible. If the filter is turned on, we basically want to eliminate adult content. The Google folks, as an example, have devoted a lot of energy to these issues, but it is not aimed directly at pornography. They focus on a broader set of issues to which pornography is a business input.

The second area is pornography versus other objectionable content, such as violence and hate speech. The bag-of-words model is most successful under two conditions: (1) when there are unambiguous words indicating relevant content and (2) when there are a few of these indicators. Pornography has these properties; probably about 40 or 50 words, most of them unambiguous, indicate pornography. Thus, the bag-of-words model is actually not so bad for this application, especially if you like over-broad filters. However, in many other areas, such as violence and hate speech, the bag-of-words model is less effective. Often you must read four or five sentences of a text before identifying it as hate speech. Accuracy becomes important in such applications, and advanced technology can be helpful here.

The third area is automated blacklisting. Remember the distinction between extensional and intentional rules; extensional rules are lists of sites that you want to block. This is an effective content-filtering technique, mostly driven by human editors now. This is a promising area for automation. Accuracy is important because blocking one site can block thousands of pages; you want to be sure of doing the right thing. Advanced text technology also can play a role here.

A potential problem with these text technologies is their lack of robustness. They can be circumvented through changes in meaning. If a pornographer wants to get through a filter that he knows and can test, then he or she will be able to get through it—it is simply a question of effort. But pornographers are not economically motivated to expend a lot of effort to get through these filters. I may be wrong, but my sense is that, because children do not pay for pornography, this is probably not a problem.

In summary, true machine-aided text understanding will not be available in the near term, and that means there always will be a significant error rate with any automated method. The advanced text technologies improve accuracy, which may be important in contexts such as free speech in libraries, identification of violence and hate speech, and automated blacklisting.

The extent of the improvement from these technologies depends on many parameters, and tests must be run.[3] The latest numbers I know of are from *Consumer Reports*,[4] but they are aggregated and not broken down

---

[3]Milo Medin said that it is difficult to do good experiments and that sloppy experimentation is rewarded in a strange way. First, you run a very large collection of text through your filter and determine how much of the material identified as pornographic was, in fact, not. Second, you find out how much of the material identified as not pornographic was, in fact, a problem. If you do that analysis badly or carelessly, your filter looks better.

[4]*Consumer Reports*, March 2001.

by area. There is probably a big difference in accuracy between pornography and the other objectionable areas. There is also a trade-off between false positives and false negatives. The extent to which advanced techniques make a difference depends on where in the trade-off you start out. If I had to give a number, I would expect a 20 to 30 percent improvement in accuracy over the bag-of-words model—if you want to let all good content through (if you do not want over-blocking).

3

Categorization of Images

David Forsyth

3.1 CHALLENGES IN OBJECT RECOGNITION

The process of determining whether a picture is pornographic involves object recognition, which is difficult for a lot of reasons. First, it is difficult to know what an object is; things look different from different angles and in different lights. When color and texture change, things look different. People can change their appearance by moving their heads around. We do not look different to one another when we do this, but we certainly look different in pictures.

The state of the art in object recognition is finding buildings in pictures taken from satellites. Computer programs sometimes can find people. We are good at finding faces. We can tell—sort of—whether a picture has nearly naked people in it. But there is no program that reliably determines whether there are people wearing clothing in a picture. The main way to look for people with clothes is to look for the ones without clothes. It is a remarkable fact of nature that virtually everyone's skin looks about the same in a picture (even across different racial groups), as long as we are careful about intensity issues. Skin is easy to detect reliably in pictures, so the first thing we look for is skin. But we need to realize that photographs of the California desert, apple pies, and all sorts of other things also have a blank color. Therefore, we need a pattern for how skin is arranged.

Long, thin bits of skin might be an arm, leg, or torso. Because the kinematics of the body is limited, certain things cannot be done with arms and legs. If I find an arm, for example, then I know where to look for a leg. If I put enough of them together, then there is a person in the picture. If there is a person and there is skin, then they have no clothes on, and there is a problem. We could reason about the arrangement of skin, or we could simply say that any big blob of skin must be a naked person. We did a classification based on kinematics.

Performance assessment is complicated. There are two things to consider: first, the probability that the program will say a picture is rude when it is not (i.e., false positive) and, second, the probability that the program will say a picture is not rude when it is (i.e., false negative). Although it is desirable to try to make both numbers as small as possible, the appropriate trade-off between false positives and false negatives depends on the application, as described below. Moreover, false positive and false negative rates can be measured in different ways. Doing the experiments can be embarrassing because a lot of pictures need to be handled and viewed, and all sorts of other things make it tricky as well. The experiments are difficult to assess because they all use different sets of data. People usually report the experiments that display their work in a good light. In view of these phenomena, it is not easy to say what would happen if we dropped one of these programs on the Web.

3.2 SCREENING OF PORNOGRAPHIC IMAGES

One way to reduce viewing of pornographic images is intimidation. A manager or parent might say to employees or children that Internet traffic will be monitored. They might explain that the image categorization program will store every image it is worried about in a folder and, once a week, the folder will be opened and the contents displayed. If the images are problematic, the manager or parent will have a conversation with the employee or child. This approach might work, because when people are warned about monitoring, they may not behave in a silly way.

But it will work only if there is a low probability of false positives. No one will pay attention to monitoring if each week 1,500 "pornographic" pictures are discovered in the folder, all being pictures of apple pies that the program has misinterpreted. The security industry usually says that people faced with many false positives get bored and do not want to deal with the problem.[1] On the other hand, a high rate of false negatives is not a concern in this context. Typically, in a monitoring application, letting

---

[1]Milo Medin noted that the Internal Revenue Service (IRS) uses the intimidation approach. In the tax context, many false positives may not be a problem. Certain behaviors cause the IRS to expend a lot of energy to respond. If the consequences of an investigation are high enough, then the IRS needs to do it only a few times to generate certain behaviors.

one or two pictures sneak in is not a problem. If there is a high false-negative rate, then we will get a warning. We might not see every one, but we will know there is an issue.

Another approach is to render every picture coming through a network. We could fill a building with banks of people looking at all the pictures and saying, "I don't like this one." This is not practical. We could take a "no porn shall pass" attitude, but then we really care whether the possibility of a false negative is small, and there is a risk that we might not know what is being left out. Large chunks of information might be ruled as objectionable by the program without, in fact, being objectionable, and we would not know about it.

Yet another approach is site classification. We could look at a series of pictures from one site, and if our program thinks that enough of them are rude, then we could say that the whole site is rude. We need to be careful about such rules, however, because of a conditional probability issue, as discussed below.

A program that I wrote with Ida Fleck marks about 40 percent of pornographic pictures, where a pornographic picture is an image that can be downloaded from an adult-oriented site. This program thinks pictures are pornographic if they contain lots of stuff that looks like skin that is in long bits and in a certain arrangement. A picture that appears to have lots of skin but in the wrong arrangement is not judged to be pornographic. Pictures with little skin showing are not identified as pornographic. But pictures of things like deserts, cabins, the Colorado plateau, cuisine, barbecue, salads, fruit, and the colors of autumn are sometimes identified as pornographic. Spatial analysis is difficult and is done poorly. The program often identifies pies as torsos. But the program is not completely worthless—it does find some naughty pictures. Sometimes the colors are not adjusted correctly, so that the skin does not look like skin, but the background does. But this seldom happens because it makes people look either seasick or dead; usually, the people who scan the film adjust the colors.

This brings up the conditional probability issue. This program is slightly better at identifying pictures of puddings than it is at detecting pictures of naked people, because an apple tart looks like skin arranged in lines and strips. Generally, if a Web page contains pictures of puddings, then the program says each picture is a problem and, therefore, the Web page is a problem. This is a common conditional probability issue that arises in different ways with different programs. There is no reason to believe that computer vision technology will eliminate it.

Mike Jones and Jim Ray did some work on skin detectors. When they found skin, they looked for a big skin blob and, if it was big enough, they said the picture was a problem. The program cannot tell if a person is wearing a little bathing costume or if the skin belongs to a dog instead of a human. They plotted the probability of a false positive against the probability of detection. If you wanted only a 4 percent probability of a false positive, for example, then you would mark about 70 percent of pornographic pictures. I am not sure whether they used as many pictures of puddings or the Colorado desert in their experiments as I did. Density also affects the results; doing these experiments right is not easy. They analyzed text as well as images. I think they used a simple bag-of-words model with perhaps some conditional probability function. To mark about 90 percent of the pornographic pictures, you would get about 8 percent false positives, which might be a very serious issue. Unless you are in the business of finding out who is looking at rude pictures, then 8 percent false alarms would be completely unacceptable.

Several things make it easier to identify pornography than you might think. First, people tend to be big in these pictures because there is not much else. There are also wild correlations among words, pictures, and links. Most porn Web sites are linked to most others. What you think about a picture should change based on where you came from on the Web.

Filtering, or at least auditing, can be done in close to real time. A Canadian product called Porn Sweeper audits in close enough to real time that the producers claim that someone transmitting or receiving large numbers of these pictures will get a knock on the door within the next day or so, rather than the next month. But this is not fast enough to meet everyone's needs.

3.3 THE FUTURE

Face detection is becoming feasible. The best systems recognize 90 percent of faces with about 5 percent false positives. This is good performance and getting much better.[2] In 3 to 5 years, the computer vision community will have many good face-detection methods. This might help in identifying pornography, because skin with a face is currently more of a problem than skin without a face. Face detection technology probably can be applied to very specific body parts; text and image data and connectivity information also will help.

---

[2]Milo Medin said that security software now on the market uses a camera in the computer to identify the user during sign on. Bob Schloss commented that it is much easier to compare an image to one or more known, authorized users than to an arbitrary person.

However, I do not believe that the academic computer vision community will be highly engaged in solving this problem, for three reasons. First, it embarrasses the funding agencies. Second, my students have been tolerant, but it is difficult to assign a job containing all sorts of problematic pictures. Third, it embarrasses and outrages colleagues, depending on their inclinations.

Technical solutions can help manage some problems. I am convinced that most practical solutions will have users in the loop somewhere. The user is not necessarily a child trying to avoid pornography; he or she may be a parent who backs up the filter and initiates a conversation when problematic pictures arise. What is almost certainly manageable, and going to become more so, is a test to determine whether there might be naked people in a picture. The intimidation scenario described above could work technically in the not too distant future.

What will remain difficult are functions such as distinguishing hardcore from soft-core pornography. These terms are used as though they mean something, but it is not clear that they do. Significant aspects of this problem are basically hopeless for now. There have been reasonable disagreements about the photographs of Jock Sturgess, for example. Many depict naked children. They are generally not felt to be prurient, but whether they are problematic is a real issue. There is no hope that a computer program will solve that issue.

Another example of a dilemma is a composite photograph prepared by someone whose intentions were clearly prurient. One side shows children on a beach looking in excited horror at the other side of the frame, where a scuba diver is exposing himself. There was a legal debate over this photo in the United Kingdom and a legal issue in this country as well. One part of the photo showed kids pointing at a jellyfish on the beach; the other part was a lad with his shorts off. Real people might believe that the intention of that photograph is prurient and seriously problematic, but there is no hope that a computer program will detect that. It is not even clear whether pictures such as this are legal or illegal in this country; reasonable people could differ on that question.

Based on my knowledge of computer vision and what appears to be practically possible, any government interested in getting around filters designed to censor things like Voice of America is wasting its money. Either that, or it is engaged in the essentially benevolent activity of supporting research. Something like this could be regarded as a final course project in information-retrieval computer vision for a statistical English program. This will remain true for the foreseeable future.

4

The Technology of Search Engines

Ray Larson

4.1 OVERVIEW

Most search engine companies do not want to reveal what their technology is or does, because they consider that to be a trade secret. Every company claims to do retrieval better than every other company, and they do not want to lose their competitive edge. I will provide a broad overview of how search technology works in current engines, based on the old standard models of information retrieval.

Two players are involved: the information system and the people who want the information stored in the system. The searchers go through a process of formulating a query, that is, describing what they seek in ways that the system can process. The same sort of thing happens on the other end, where the system has to extract information from the documents included in its database. Those documents need to be described in such a way that someone posing a query can find them.

In general, the emphasis in the design and development of search engines has been to make the document finding process as effective as possible—today, however the goal seems to be to exclude some searchers. The idea is to prevent some people from getting things that we think they should not get. This is anathema to someone from a library background, where we tend to think that everyone should have access to everything and that it is up to Mom and Dad to say no.

In between the information system and the searcher are the search engine's processing functions (the "rules of the game")—how the languages are structured, all the information that can be acquired from the documents that come in, and how that gets mapped to what a searcher wants. The usual outcome is a set of potentially relevant documents. The searcher does not know whether a retrieved document is really relevant until he or she looks at it and says, "Yes, that is what I wanted."

Much of what happens in search engines, which generally use the "bag-of-words" model for handling data, is structure recognition. Search engines often treat titles differently than they do the body of a Web page; titles indicate the topic of a page. If the system can extract structure from documents, it often can be used as an indicator for additionally weighting the retrieval process.

Often the search engine normalizes the text, stripping out capitalization and most other orthographic differences among words. Some systems do not throw this information away automatically but rather attempt to identify things such as sequences of capitalized words possibly indicating a place or person's name. The search engine then usually removes stop words, a list of words that it chooses not to index. This would be a likely place to put a filter. But this can become problematic because, when using a bag-of-words model, one occurrence of a word does not indicate other nonproblematic occurrences of the same word. If the usual suspect words were placed on the list of stop words, then suddenly the American Kennel Club Web site no longer would be accessible, because of all of the words that refer to the gender of female dogs, and so on. Rarely, the search engine also may apply natural language processing (NLP) to identify known phrases or chunks of text that properly belong together and indicate certain types of content.

4.2 BOOLEAN SEARCH LOGIC

What is left is a collection of words that need to be retrieved in some way. There are many models for doing this. The simplest and most widely available—used in virtually every search engine and the initial commercial search model—is the Boolean operator model. Simple Boolean logic says either "this word *and* that word occur," or "this word *or* that word occur," and, therefore, the documents that have those words should be retrieved. Boolean logic is simple and easy to implement. Almost all search engines today, because of the volume of data on the Internet, include an automatic default setting that, in effect, uses the AND operator with all terms provided to the search engine. If the searcher turns this function off, then the search engine usually defaults to a ranking algorithm that attempts to do a "best match" for the query.

All of these combinations can be characterized in a simple logic model that says that this word either occurs in the document or that it does not. If it does occur, you have certain matches; if not, you have other matches.

Any combination of three words, for example, can be specified, such that the document has this word and not the other two, or all three together, or one and not the other of two. You can specify any combination of the words. But if you do not specify the word *exactly* as it is stored in the index, then you will not get it. It cannot be a synonym (unless you supply that synonym), or an alternative phrasing, or a euphemism.

4.3 THE VECTOR SPACE MODEL

Another approach is the vector space model. This model was developed over 30 years of intensive research into a finely honed set of tools. Probabilistic models are also being used much more commonly these days. Many other models combine many of the same aspects, including attempts to automatically recognize structures of information within documents that would indicate relevance. Alternatively, one could look at all of the documents in a collection and consider each individual word that occurs in any of those documents. But most large collections have tens of thousands of words, even hundreds of thousands. A large proportion of those words are nonsense, misspellings, or other problems that occur once or twice, whereas other words occur often (e.g., the, and, of).

The vector space model attempts to consider each term that occurs in a document as if it were a dimension in Euclidean space. (This is why we use three terms as an example; if there are more than three dimensions, it becomes difficult for people to think about.) In a vector space model, each document has a vector that points in a certain direction, depending on whether it contains a term or not. The documents are differentiated on this basis. This example shows a system where there is a simple yes/no process; a document either has the term or does not have it. You also can consider each term as having a particular weight, which can be measured in a variety of ways, such as how frequently the word occurs in a particular document.

In this model, you are calculating the cosine of the angle between two vectors in imaginary space. The smaller the angle between the vectors, the more similar the document is to the query. You can rank documents based on that closeness or similarity.[1] Therefore, in most vector space models, you do not need to match all the words. As long as you match

---

[1] Nick Belkin said that similarity in text documents is relatively easy to compute, assuming constant meaning of words, whereas similarity of images is very difficult to compute. David Forsyth gave the example of the Pope kissing a baby versus a picture of a politician kissing a baby; they are the same picture in some ways, but different in others.

many or even some of the words, you will get closer to a particular document that has those words in it.

This model uses "term frequency/inverse document frequency" (TF-IDF), a measure of the frequency of occurrence of a particular term in a particular document, as well as how often that term occurs in the entire collection of interest. If a term occurs frequently in one document but also occurs frequently in every other document in the collection, then it is not a very important word, and the TF-IDF measure reduces the weight placed on it. A common term is considered less important than rare terms. If a term occurs in every document, then the inverse document frequency is zero; if it occurs in half of the documents, it will be 0.3; and if it occurs in 20 of 10,000 documents, it will be 2.6. If a term occurs in just one document, then the IDF measure would be 4—the highest weight possible. Unfortunately, most pornographic words, given the distribution of porn on the Internet, are not rare.

Once you have extracted the words from the documents, you have to put the words somewhere. They usually are placed in an inverted file, which puts the words into a list with an indication of which documents they came from. Then the list is sorted to get all the terms in alphabetical order, and duplicates are merged; if there are multiple entries for a particular document or term, then you increment the frequency for that item. This is the simplest form of an inverted file. Many search engines also keep track of where a word occurs in a document, to provide proximity information. They also keep track of many other things, such as how many links there are to the page that a word is on.

Finally, you differentiate the file to make a unique list for every term that occurs in the entire database, with pointers that say in which documents they occurred and how frequently. With that information, you can then calculate the magical-looking formulas that provide a ranking for a document.

4.4 SEARCHING THE WORLD WIDE WEB

Most Web search engines use versions of the vector space model and also offer some sort of Boolean ranking. Some search engines use probabilistic techniques as well. Others do little more than a coordination-level matching, looking for documents that have the highest number of specified terms. Some use natural language processing (Lycos, for example, was based on some NLP work by Michael Mauldin). Excite's concept-based search may be a development of Latent Semantic Indexing (developed at Bell Labs). The Inktomi search engine formerly used a form of retrieval based on logistic regression.

Virtually all search engines use the bag-of-words of model.² Some use additional page weight methods, looking not only at frequency of a word in a document, but also at other things like the number of links to a page. Google uses in-links, for example. If no one links to your page, then you would get a lower rank than someone who had the same words but many in-links. Most search engines also include every string of characters on a page, even if they are total garbage. Therefore, in addition to comparing one word to another, you have to compare all of the numbers, which is difficult.

Exact algorithms are not available for most commercial Web search engines. Most search engines appear to be hybrids of rank and Boolean searching. They allow you to do a guess-match symbolized by the vector space model and also very strict Boolean matching. But most users never click to the "advanced search" page, which explains how to do all of these things; they usually just type in what they think would be an appropriate search. Most people looking at search logs would say, "That's ridiculous. How are they ever going to find anything?"

The search engine obtains this material by sending out a "spider" to retrieve the pages from Web sites. They retrieve only static pages, not pages that are hiding as databases or are dynamically generated. Most crawlers also obey the robot.txt file on a Web site; if the file says, "Do not index this site," they do not index that site. They can store millions of words and hundreds of sites.

There are different methods of crawling. In a depth-first crawl, you go down as deep as you can within any particular site before going on to the next site. Another way is a breadth-first search, where you start across many different sites and work your way down slowly.³ Part of the reason

---

²David Forsyth observed that it might be logical to ask why people use the bag-of-words model, which they know to be bad. The answer is, it is very difficult to use anything else. Most reasonable people know about 60,000 words. You need to count how often each one appears in text. You need a lot of text to do this. If you are modeling the probability of seeing a new word, given an old word, there are 60,000 choices for the old word and 60,000 choices for the new word. The table would be 60,000 by 60,000, and it would be difficult to collect enough data to fill the table. Ray Larson noted that 60,000 words is a very small size compared to the indexes used by search engines.

³Nick Belkin noted that a crawler is limited by the size of its own memory. As soon as it finds as much as it can hold, it stops. Milo Medin observed that this is not an ideal approach. Rather, you want to rank order the types of things that you will either archive or not. If you cannot store all the useful things, then, rather than stop, a better approach is to go back and prune out some of the duplicate or irrelevant material. Ray Larson said finding duplicates is a big deal, because many things either have the same name or have different names but are on the same pages. For database storage and efficiency reasons, it is important to find those things.

for this is, if a spider comes to your Web site and hits you 50,000 times in a row to get every single page that you have, you will get upset. Instead, breadth-first spiders spread out the hits over time among a number of sites. The main message here is that the pages have to be connected somehow to the starting points or else you never will get them—that is, unless someone has sent you a pointer saying, "Here is the new starting point. Here's our site, please index it."[4] Some people sell algorithms that ensure that a given page gets ranked higher than others. Search engine companies spend a lot of their time figuring out how to identify and counteract the "spammed" pages from those people. It is an "arms race."[5]

A paper published in *Nature* in 1999 estimated the types of material indexed, excluding commercial sites.[6] Scientific and educational sites were the largest population. Health sites, personal sites, and the sites for societies (scholarly or other) are all larger than the percentage estimated for pornography.[7] No search engine has 100 percent coverage, and they often cover quite different things. There can be overlap, as well. There are also issues of numbers of links. If one site indexes something, then

---

[4]Milo Medin said that some sites generate indexes by asking other search engines and indexing what they already have. He also said that no catalog inventories show up in searches because the inventory is designed for a database query. The exception is when that site has created an index page with a set of stored queries.

[5]Winnie Wechsler said that there seems to be a fundamental tension between search engines striving to provide the greatest accuracy to users in terms of retrieval or filtering and Web publishers trying to trick or mislead the search engines to make sure their sites are listed as much and as high in rank as possible. How does this tension resolve itself? It does not seem resolvable, certainly in the case of pornography. Nick Belkin said one approach is to use more words in a query to make the conditions more restrictive. A query with 10 words will get a much better result than one with only 2 words because it defines much more context. The difficulty is that, even though the average number of words per query on the Web has been going up, it is still only about 2.3 words, up from 1.7 words a few years ago. With very simple search engine technology, it may help to encourage people to use more words in their queries.

[6]Steve Lawrence and C. Lee Giles, "Accessibility and Distribution of Information on the Web," *Nature* 400(6740): 107-109, July 8, 1999.

[7]Milo Medin said that the declining cost of Web serving—generally a good thing—has made it easier for amateur pornographers to get published. Medin's service offers free Web hosting for a certain amount of material. Subscribers are not allowed to post pornography or objectionable material, but there is no cost or punishment if they do, so they take advantage of this situation. The company audits sites based on the amount of traffic to them. When a site attracts a certain amount of traffic, it triggers a red flag and generates a query to the people in charge of investigating abuse. Medin recalled that, when he worked for NASA, data on international links had to be controlled. When someone put up a porn site, the link utilization to that region would rise. A wiretap would reveal where the traffic was going.

another site will index it. Things that are unique tend to stay unique within a particular search engine.[8]

In looking for images, text retrieval technology looks for text that is associated with images. It looks for an image link tag within the HTML and the sentences that surround it on either side. This can be highly deceptive. The words "Oh, look at the cute bunnies" mean one thing on a children's Web site and something entirely different on Playboy's site. Thus, the words alone may not indicate what those images are about.

---

[8]Milo Medin emphasized the business dynamic, noting that creating the search capability to find an obscure Web page may not be worth the cost in terms of its impact on the subscriber base. Say a search engine fails to find 5 percent of the material on the Internet. To some people whose content is in that 5 percent, this is important. But if the cost of finding that 5 percent is double the cost of finding the other 95 percent and the bulk of searchers are satisfied with that performance, it may not be worth it. Search engines are not librarians; they exist for a business purpose.

5

Cyber Patrol: A Major Filtering Product

Susan Getgood

5.1 INTRODUCTION

SurfControl, Inc., is the world's largest filtering company, with offices and companies throughout the world. The company attained this position through a combination of organic growth and growth by acquisition. In 1998 it got into the corporate filtering business, and in 1998 and 2000 it acquired both SurfWatch and Cyber Patrol, the pioneers in filtering to protect kids from inappropriate content.

I will tell you what filtering software is and what it is not. It is safety technology, like a seatbelt for Internet surfing. Seatbelts are not 100 percent guaranteed to save a child's life, but there is no responsible parent in America who does not buckle up a child in the car. We believe the situation is the same in protecting kids from inappropriate content online. Filtering software puts the choice of how and when children can use the Web in the hands of the people who should have it: parents and educators. It is also the most effective way to safeguard kids from inappropriate Web content without compromising First Amendment rights, which is important. We are creating a solution that puts choice in the hands of the people who need it, while keeping the government out of those choices.

Filtering software is not a replacement for the guidance of parents and educators. I doubt any filtering software company would suggest that parents, teachers, educators, administrators, business people, or anyone use filtering software without clearly providing the guidance that children need to understand what they see on the Internet.

Web filtering products either block or allow access to Web sites by either IP addresses or domain names. Most of the widely available commercial products are list based, with human reviewers. These products also use some artificial intelligence (AI) tools but not as the primary mechanism of filtering. Technologies work for us in the research process, but they do not replace human review, which verifies that the content on a page is about, for example, a marijuana joint and not the Joint Chiefs of Staff, or that a woman in a picture is not wearing a tan bathing suit. We need human reviewers to make sure that content really is inappropriate.

5.2 WHY FILTER?

About 30 million children in this country have access to the Internet, and about 25 percent of them are exposed to some type of unwanted or inappropriate online content. Although we are mostly concerned here with sexually explicit content and pornography, it is important to remember that parents and educators are concerned about broader types of content, from hate sites and intolerance material to how to build a bomb and buy a gun. Parents and educators are the people with whom I deal most in my job, which is running the Cyber Patrol brand.

Parents want this type of technology and they want it used both in schools and at home. In 2000, a study by Digital Media found that 92 percent of Americans want some type of filtering to be used in schools; they are concerned about the content that their children see. Our job is to find a way to make filtering an effective technology solution that does not get in the way of the educational experience, whether at home or in school.

Interestingly, we found that people do not always realize there is a problem until they look at their hard drives and find Miss April or Miss May. As reported in the press recently, a teacher (a customer of one of our competitors) checked the history of each computer and was appalled at what the students were able to access. They were accessing sexually explicit material, gambling, applying for credit cards, buying products without parents' permission—a whole host of things. There is clearly a problem out there in the world, and parents and schools want to do something about it.

Corporations filter for four basic reasons: (1) productivity of employees; (2) legal liability for inappropriate content being available on networks; (3) issues of inappropriate surfing, which takes up room in the information pipeline; and (4) increasing demand for security to prevent compromise of confidential information. In schools, we tend to focus on filtering to protect children from inappropriate content. But we have found that network bandwidth increasingly is an issue in schools, especially with respect to federal mandates for filters, which we oppose. We believe that schools purchase filtering software because it solves a wide variety of problems, not just the simple, single problem of protecting kids from inappropriate content.

We mailed a quick e-mail survey out last week to 1,200 customers and got a 2.64 percent response rate, which is fairly good in this time frame. We asked them how important Internet bandwidth was to them last year versus this year. Fifty-five percent said it was very important or important last year, compared to 70 percent this year. Similarly, 37 percent were either neutral or thought it was an unimportant issue last year, compared to only 24 percent this year. This is what our customers are telling us, both anecdotally and numerically. The bandwidth issue arises when kids in the library go off to look at Napster,[1] free e-mail accounts like hot mail and Yahoo mail, and anything else not on task. Even something otherwise appropriate, such as checking out sports scores, is not on task at work or school. If Napster is regulated, something else will come along to replace it as the next big thing on the Internet. We try to stay ahead of what our customers need, and Internet developments like Napster prove to me that educators are looking at the whole issue of managing the Internet in the classroom, not just the management of sexually explicit content.

5.3 SUPERSCOUT AND CYBER PATROL

We have two brands, SuperScout and Cyber Patrol. I will describe SuperScout briefly and then concentrate on Cyber Patrol.

SuperScout was developed to do filtering, monitoring, or reporting in a corporate environment. It uses an extensive list of nonbusiness-related Web sites. It has an optional AI tool that provides dynamic classification of content, looking at the sites employees visit. Some sites are on the SurfControl list, and some are not. If a site is not on the list, then the AI program uses pattern recognition and textual analysis. It can run this information against the category definitions of the business product and give the corporation an additional list that can act as a buffer against the content that people actually see. We do not plan to add this technology to the home filtering products, although we use it in research before the reviewers look at something. We see a trend, especially in institutional settings but also in homes, toward managing access to the content that people actually are trying to see—as opposed to having huge category lists of which employees are trying to access only 1 percent.

---

[1] Milo Medin said that the bandwidth issue is driven primarily by multimedia. Many Internet service providers have issues with Napster traffic; about 10-15 percent of bandwidth traffic on his company's interconnects is Napster traffic.

Cyber Patrol, which keeps kids safe, comes in stand-alone versions for the home and network versions for schools. The network version operates either on local area networks or through proxy servers. Cyber Patrol for schools focuses on blocking Web access, and it goes through the Microsoft proxy server, Microsoft Internet Security and Acceleration Server 2000, or Novell Border Manager. We incorporate elements within the software that address the whole scope of what parents are trying to do to protect their kids. We enhanced security and improved tamper resistance in the latest version for the home. Parents can customize settings for multiple children or multiple grades. We also provide information about why a site is blocked, so that parents can explain to their children why they were not allowed to access something.

Cyber Patrol works the same way if you are a subscriber to America Online (AOL). Typically it is used in addition to AOL's parental controls, which are based on work that we did. Other Internet service providers also offer these types of controls. An advantage to using a stand-alone filter is that it works regardless of how children access the Internet. It follows the same set of rules regardless of whether a child uses AOL, your dial-up modem to work, or a dial-up modem they got from a friend, because the software is installed on the computer. We have many customers who use AOL but also use Cyber Patrol specifically because they want the same settings and time management across multiple services.

Server-based filters, the primary design used in schools and businesses, tend to be integrated with networks and users. When you log in as Jimmy Smith in the seventh grade, the filter knows that you are Jimmy Smith and how to apply the filtering rules. Different rules can be applied for different users within a school system. In our user base, school districts have different rules in elementary school versus middle school versus high school—except for sexually explicit material, which tends to be blocked throughout the whole school system. As an example, you may not want the fourth graders to access material about intolerance, but the seventh graders may be doing a project on hate groups. (Setting rules in different ways is consistent with the new law against disabling filters.) Eventually, as student identification (ID) cards move toward becoming smart cards, a child's filter rules, lunch money, and library books will all be on the ID card.[2]

---

[2]Milo Medin said that user identification and sign-on always have been complicated because they involve sharing a password. But fingerprint scanners are becoming less expensive and are starting to appear in keyboards. This enables a user-friendly level of identification, because you no longer need to worry about getting your password right. This will become more common in the marketplace.

We block lists of specific pages (identified by their uniform resource locator designations (URLs)); we do not analyze the content of a page as it is downloaded to a subscriber's computer. Playboy.com is blocked because it is Playboy, not because the program senses nude pictures or forbidden words. We can block an entire site or by page level. Cyber Patrol for homes is based on a list called the CyberNOT List, reviewed in its entirety by human reviewers. Our team of professional researchers is made up of parents and teachers. Parents can then select the categories of lists that they want to use. We tailor the filtering levels to meet the needs of different children. Age-appropriate filtering is possible; for example, we have a sex education category so that material that otherwise would be considered sexually explicit can be made available to older children en masse.

There are 13 CyberNOT categories to choose from: violence and profanity, partial nudity, full nudity, sexual acts, gross depictions, intolerance, satanic and cult, alcohol and drugs, alcohol and tobacco, drugs and drug culture, militant and extremist, sex education, and questionable/illegal material and material related to gambling. The definitions are published on our Web site and in the product itself, so that parents can review the definitions as they decide how to tailor the software's settings to fit their needs. About 70-80 percent of the list content is violence or profanity, partial nudity, full nudity, sexual acts, and gross depictions. The other categories make up 20-30 percent; these categories are more difficult to research and much less obvious.

We publish our content definitions and categories. We give you the ability to override or allow based on your own preferences, but we do not publish the sites that are on our category list. We have spent thousands of dollars to build a proprietary list that cannot be duplicated by anyone; I have yet to hear a commercial reason that makes sense why we should allow that. As a company devoted to protecting kids from inappropriate content, we will not publish a directory of dirty sites.

We do not filter URLs or Web sites by keyword, which is an important point. We do use keywords as part of the research process to get suspect material to look at. The training process is done on the job using a shadowing technique. That is, a new researcher works with someone who has been doing it for a while to understand the process. Researchers work in teams, which is important in identifying material, particularly when the material is difficult to classify and a discussion about it is helpful. Most researchers have child development backgrounds, typically with some type of training, whether teaching certification or on-the-job-training as a parent. They are not child development specialists or psychologists, but they have an appreciation for why and how to classify the material.

Cyber Patrol does not interfere with, or get involved in, the search engine process. The software works purely in the browsing process. We can block a search on sex if that is what the parent wishes, but we do not filter search results. If a child tries to visit a blocked site, Cyber Patrol shows you that the site does exist but that you were not allowed to access it, and tells the parent why. If you are trying to make this site available for your family, you can go back and change that particular site's setting and know that you are fixing the right thing, as opposed to stumbling around blindly, trying to figure out why a site was blocked.

We deal with two kinds of chat. One is Web-based chat, which we block specifically by blocking the category of Web-based chat. Alternatively, you can use privacy features, which allow kids to go into chat rooms—if you want them to be allowed to talk about bird watching or whatever—but not to give out their names, addresses, or phone numbers. It cannot do anything about a 15-year-old who is determined to tell someone his address. But if a naive 12-year-old inadvertently gives out his number, then the feature replaces it with a set of nonsense characters. We also can block Internet relay chat, which is used much less often now than in the past, either completely or based on the chat channel name.

SurfControl gets a lot of feedback from customers. When a customer asks us to look at a site to see if it should be blocked for the larger population, not just for his or her own family, we spend more time on it than we otherwise might. Often, however, such sites do not warrant being added to a list that a large population uses.

Consumers can decide how well we make decisions by trying the product before they buy it.[3] Parents using Cyber Patrol can try to go to a Web site that is blocked and, if they think it should not be blocked, bypass the filter and look at the site and make a personal decision about whether Cyber Patrol was right or wrong in putting that site on the list. (Parents can override the system, but children cannot, because, hopefully, they do not have the necessary password. Picking the family dog's name as the password is probably not a good idea.) There is an element of trust. If they believe that we offer them a good place to start—filtering software is not a replacement for parents, nor is it a solution for everything—then it is a reasonable place to start to protect their kids. We try to provide parents with a solution that gives them the ability to implement their own choices.

---

[3]David Forsyth argued that it is easy to determine whether a dishwasher works because the plates either come out clean or dirty, but it is difficult to tell whether Cyber Patrol works, so the choice issue becomes problematic. Milo Medin noted that the average housewife is not likely to figure out the difference between good and poor dishwashing fluid. Rather, she makes decisions based on brand, consumer reports, and other evaluations. Medin said he does not make decisions about highly technical matters based only on his own experiments; third parties do these lab tests.

We cannot guarantee 100 percent true positives, but we do the best job we can to build the tool. If there is a metric for deciding how much accuracy is enough, it is the market. The market decides what level of accuracy it wants by making product choices. If we have a good product, then presumably parents, schools, and businesses will continue to buy it. If we did not have a good product, then I truly believe that Joe in his garage would come up with something better.

One reason why we oppose mandatory filtering is that we believe the use of these products should be a choice that parents and educators make, just as it is a choice for businesses. When you select and evaluate a product—in our case, you can try it for 14 days before you buy it—then the choice is yours. If it is mandated, then it is not a choice.

5.4 THE REVIEW PROCESS

To clarify, we have two review processes. One is the process of finding new material that comes onto the Internet. We use a variety of mechanisms, from search engines to crawlers. That same group of people is involved in the re-review process to make sure that once something is on the list, it should remain on the list.

The Cyber Patrol team consists of about 10 people; most have been with us for at least 2 years and some more than 4 years. It is a good job for a parent who wants a part-time or supplementary job. We have worked hard to ensure that the job entails more than just looking at inappropriate content all day, which would be absolutely mind numbing. We also build positive lists. We have a Yes list that we use. The job also has responsibility in the technical side of building these lists.

It might sound like a great job, looking at porn all day. But after about a day, it becomes less fun. To understand what they are reading, the reviewers can spend anywhere from a minute or less on pornographic material to upwards of 10 minutes on intolerance material or something that requires textual analysis. A sexually explicit site can be judged fairly quickly; a picture is a picture. If deeper probing into a site is required, that takes longer. We do not block sites simply because they do mousetrapping,[4] and we do not view this technique as a red flag for sites to be reviewed. (I plan on suggesting it, however.)

---

[4]Mousetrapping—a technique in which clicking on an item causes a second item to pop up—is used by pornography and gambling sites. Milo Medin said that he would pay for blocking of sites that use mouse trapping, especially when it has multiple levels. Herb Lin noted that the underlying technology has legitimate purposes, such as in making surveys or questionnaires pop up on consumer sites.

It is a mistake to attribute political motives to SurfControl or any other major filtering company. We add sites to our list based on their content. In the case of the gossip site The Register,[5] my understanding is that it published a detailed explanation of how people could use a loophole in anonymous proxies to get around the use of filtering software—to let kids get pornography. This is why the site was added to the list.[6] The ultimate example of a difficult case might be determining whether an image is art or nudity. We would not consider work by Rubins Wake to be nudity, because it is art. However, if you duplicated one of those images on your own personal Web page, using your own friends and family, then that probably would not qualify as art.

We make sure that we re-review material, so that Web sites that go out of existence do not stay on our list. We have regular re-reviews of the list categories, both as projects within the research department and as part of the customer feedback process. On average, we probably cycle through the whole CyberNot List about once every year. Some categories get more frequent reviews. We look at some sites every month. A couple of organizations ask us to look at sites every month, and we do. After the Heaven's Gate incident,[7] we made an effort to go back through all the material on the cult. The same thing was done after the Columbine High School shooting.[8] We do re-reviews of the categories that are particularly relevant to these sorts of issues. The software comes with a year's subscription to daily updates, so it is updated on a regular basis.

We are looking at AI to speed up some of the review processes. One approach is dynamic pattern matching. Internal tests reveal up to 85 percent accuracy or agreement between what our reviewers find and what the tool finds. As that number starts to improve, we will be able to start relying more on this tool. Right now we do not believe that eliminating the human review process in Cyber Patrol is the right thing to do.

Here are two paraphrases of what reviewers say about their jobs. They take this job very seriously, which is one reason why we have been able to keep some of these people for upwards of 4 or 5 years. They really

---

[5]David Forsyth said The Register claimed it was blocked because it had said the financial basis of the filtering market was not as sound as it looked and that SurfControl might be taken over.

[6]David Forsyth said that this is a situation in which a legitimate discussion of a technological issue was cut short because useful, retrievable information was taken out of the public domain. Susan Getgood said that the company does not claim it never makes mistakes and that perhaps the researcher who added the site to the list was being overzealous.

[7]In March 1997, 39 members of the Heaven's Gate cult committed suicide.

[8]In April 1999, two students went on a shooting spree in their suburban high school in Jefferson County, Colorado. Thirteen people were killed and 21 were wounded.

do believe that they are doing something that helps parents do their job better.

- "Being a researcher demands an open mind and an objective outlook at all times. We try to protect children and many adults from offensive and harmful material without encroaching on anyone's right to free speech."
- "It can be both difficult and rewarding. At times, seeing the worst of what is on the Internet can be difficult, but the reward comes when you know that a small child, whose parents are responsible enough to use filtering, will not ever have to see what I just saw when I put it in the database."

5.5 THE FUTURE

As part of SurfControl, we take advantage of an active research and development department. We now have 40 researchers around the world, an increase from the time when Cyber Patrol alone had 10. This gives us an ability to deal with international content in a cultural context, rather than as Americans looking at something in German or Dutch or Spanish. We are looking at the next generation of filtering and what we need to continue to do to build these products. We do not create the need for these products; the need is out there. We are doing our best to develop software and products that meet the need.

Forty reviewers might seem like a small number if you were starting today.[9] If you started this year and tried to do the whole Web in 365 days, you probably would have a tough time. But we have been doing this for 6 years, so there is a base that we are not repeating. We focus on the inappropriate content; we do not try to look at every single page on the Internet. To increase accuracy in dealing with material that is difficult to categorize, it is not a question of hiring more people but rather of looking at tools such as image recognition. We can manage the human costs and also improve the front-end part of the research.

Clearly, there will be more bandwidth to homes in the future. This will allow us to use more robust AI technologies in these products. Commands such as "Don't show me more like this one" rely on dynamic categorization. Modems cannot handle this effectively; you need high-speed,

---

[9]Marilyn Mason said that there are more than 1 billion sites total. Winnie Wechsler said that a couple of million new sites are added each year. David Forsyth said that, given 1 million new Web sites a year (not an unreasonable number), then 40 reviewers have to review 25 sites an hour in a busy year to get them all done.

broadband connections. Image filtering also is clearly part of the future, but there is not, as yet, a solution for this. We think the use of filtering also will be changed by e-mail, which is now available to just about everyone, and instant messaging. We will start looking at how to incorporate ways to keep these methods safe for kids.

Privacy is of great interest to us, because protecting kids' private information goes hand-in-hand with protecting them from inappropriate content. We already pay attention to both children's rights for privacy and parents' decisions about their children's privacy. We chose not to put a logging or monitoring feature into the Cyber Patrol home product because children have a right to privacy if they are looking at appropriate material. As rules on privacy preferences—rules about going to Web sites that collect information on kids—become finalized, we will be able to implement those rules in a technological fashion, so that parents can prevent kids from going to Web sites that, for example, publish surveys. We will be able to implement those types of things—if the market wants them.

6

Advanced Techniques for Automatic Web Filtering

Michel Bilello

6.1 BACKGROUND

As of 1999, the Web had about 16 million servers, 800 million pages, and 15 terabytes of text (comparable to the text held by the Library of Congress). By 2001, the Web was expected to have 3 billion to 5 billion pages.[1]

To prevent kids from looking at inappropriate material, one solution is to have dedicated, pornography-free Web sites—such as Yahoo!Kids and disney.com—and assign reviewers to look at those particular Web sites. This is useful in protecting children too young to know how to use a Web browser.

Filtering is mostly text based (e.g., Net Nanny, Cyber Patrol, CYBERSitter). There are different methods and problems; for example, Cyber Patrol looks at Web sites but has to update its lists all the time. You can also block keywords, scanning the pages and matching the words with keywords. But keyword blocking is usually not enough, because text embedded in images is not recognized as text.[2] You could block all images, but then surfing an imageless Web would become boring, especially for children. A group at the Nippon Electronic Corporation (NEC)

---

[1]Steve Lawrence and C. Lee Giles, "Accessibility and Distribution of Information on the Web," *Nature* 400(6740): 107-109, July 8, 1999.

[2]Michel Bilello said that his group has used a technique that pulls text off images, such as chest X-rays used for research purposes. They process the x-ray image, detect the text, and then remove, for example, the name of the patient, which the researcher does not need to know.

tried to recognize the clustering communities within the Web. You could, for example, keep the user away from particular communities or exclude some communities from the allowed Web sites.

6.2 THE WIPE SYSTEM

In the Stanford WIPE system,[3] we use software to analyze image content and make classification decisions as to whether an image is appropriate or not. Speed and accuracy are issues; for example, we try to avoid both false positives and false negatives. The common image-processing challenges to be overcome include nonuniform image background; textual noise in foreground; and a wide range of image quality, camera positions, and composition.

This work was inspired by the Fleck-Forsyth-Bregler System at the University of California at Berkeley, which classifies images as pornographic or not.[4] The published results were 52 percent sensitivity (i.e., 48 percent false negatives) and 96 percent specificity (i.e., 4 percent false positives). The Berkeley system had a rather long processing time of 6 minutes per image.

In comparison, the WIPE system has higher sensitivity, 96 percent, and somewhat less specificity (but still high) at 91 percent, and the processing time is less than 1 second per image. This technology is most applicable to automated identification of commercial porn sites; it also could be purchased by filtering companies and added to their products to increase accuracy.

In the WIPE system, the image is acquired, feature extraction is performed using wavelet technology, and, if the image is classified as a photograph (versus drawing), extra processing is done to compare a feature vector with prestored vectors. Then the image is classified as either pornographic or not, and the user can reject it or let it pass on that basis. There is an assumption that only photographs—and not manually generated images, such as an artist's rendering—would be potentially objectionable. Manually generated images can be distinguished on the basis of tones: smooth tones for manually generated images versus continuous tones for photographs. Again, only photographs would require the next processing stage.

---

[3]For a technical discussion, see James Z. Wang, *Integrated Region-based Image Retrieval*, Dordrecht, Holland: Kluwer Academic Publishers, 2001, pp. 107-122. The acronym WIPE stands for Wavelet Image Pornography Elimination.

[4]Margaret Fleck, David Forsyth, and Chris Bregler, "Finding Naked People," *Proceedings of the European Conference on Computer Vision*, B. Buxton and R. Cipolla, eds., Berlin, Germany: Springer-Verlag, Vol. 2, 1996, pp. 593-602.

This work was based on an information-retrieval system that finds in a database all the images "close" to one selected image. From the selected image the software looks at thousands of images stored in the database and retrieves all the ones that are deemed "close" to the selected image. The images were tested against a set of 10,000 photographic images and a knowledge base. The knowledge base was built with a training system. For every image there is some trusted element, a feature vector can be defined that encompasses all the information, texture, color, and so on. Then images are classified according to the information in this vector.

The database contains thousands of objectionable images of various types and thousands of benign images[5] of various types. In the training process, you process random images to see if the detection and classification are correct. You can adjust sensitivity parameters to allow tighter or looser filtering. You could combine text and images or do multiple processing of multiple images on one site to decrease the overall error in classifying a site as objectionable or not.

A statistical analysis was done showing that, if you download 20-35 images for each site, and 20-25 percent of downloaded images are objectionable, then you can classify the Web site as objectionable with 97 percent accuracy.[6] Image content analysis can be combined with text and IP address filtering. To avoid false positives, especially for art images, you can skip images that are associated with the IP addresses of museums, dog shows, beach towns, sports events, and so on.

In summary, you cannot expect perfect filtering. There is always a trade-off between performance and processing effort. But the performance of the WIPE system shows that good results can be obtained with current technology. The performance can improve by combining image-based and text-based processing. James Wang is working on training the system automatically as it extracts the features and then classifying the images manually as either objectionable and not.[7]

---

[5]To develop a set of benign images, David Forsyth suggested obtaining the Corel collection or some similar set of images known to be not-problematic or visiting Web news groups, where it is virtually guaranteed that images will not be objectionable. He said this is a rare case in which you can take a technical position without much trouble.

[6]David Forsyth took issue with the statistical analysis, because there is a conditional probability assumption that the error is independent of the numbers. In the example given earlier with images of puddings (in Forsyth's talk in Chapter 3), a large improvement in performance cannot be expected because there are certain categories in which the system will just get it wrong again. If it is wrong about one picture of pudding and then wrong again about a second picture of pudding, then it will classify the Web site wrong, also.

[7]For more information, see <http://WWW-DB.Stanford.EDU/IMAGE> (papers) and <http://wang.ist.psu.edu>.

7

A Critique of Filtering

Bennett Haselton

7.1 INTRODUCTION

I have been running the Peacefire.org site for about 5 years, and we have become known as a source of mostly critical information about blocking software and filtering. I am biased in general against the idea of filtering, as well as the existing limitations, but that is fair because all intelligent people should have opinions about what they study. They simply need to design the experiments so that the person with the opinion will not influence the outcome.

The earlier presentations provided a general idea of how different types of programs work. Some programs examine the text on a downloaded page to look for keywords in the Web page address (the uniform resource locator, or URL) or in the body of the page. Other programs are mainly list based; they do little analysis of the text on a page but have a built-in list of sites that are blocked automatically. All the programs that I know of are some combination of the two types. They have some keyword filtering and some list filtering, but they can be slotted easily into one of these categories.

Most mainstream commercial programs, such as Cyber Patrol, Net Nanny, and SurfWatch, are list based. People often talk about a scenario in which a site might get blocked if the word "sex" is in the title or first paragraph. This scenario has not been accurate for years. Sites can be blocked inaccurately, but this is not a correct way to describe what happens, because the most popular programs that look at words on the page also work off built-in lists of sites.

7.2 DEFICIENCIES IN FILTERING PROGRAMS

The mainstream commercial programs used in the home—which filter and block pages on the fly (not for auditing or later review)—do not filter images. We did a study involving the only commercial program at the time that claimed to filter images on the fly, using 50 pornographic images taken from the Web and 50 nonpornographic images. We found that the software performed no better than random chance if the images were placed in a location that the software did not know about in advance. All the pornographic and nonpornographic images in the test remained accessible, so the claim of filtering based on image contents turned out not to be true.

The company later came out with some fixes so that the program began to filter based on skin tone, but it could not do complex object recognition. The best it could do was to count the number of pixels in the picture that were skin toned and then block based on that. We did another test involving the 50 pornographic images and 50 nonpornographic pictures of people's faces, and the software scored exactly the same for each type; it was not able to tell the difference.

CYBERSitter is mostly a content-based program. Cyber Patrol is mainly a list-based program. The content-based programs are notorious for errors that arise if you block sites based on keywords on the page or in the URL. It is nowhere near as advanced as the vector space model described earlier. Yet, even though these programs are so sloppy, the examples of what they block are not very controversial, because the company justifiably can say it has no control in advance over what will be blocked. There is a certain phrase in the word filter, and if a site uses that phrase, then it is not really the company's fault. Blocking software got a bad reputation initially because of examples like a page about the exploration of Mars being blocked because the title was "Mars Explore," or mars*ex*pl.html.

I have a friend named Frank who made a Web page about Cyber Patrol, and he later found that his page was blocked—not because he was criticizing the software, but because his name was Frank, and "ank" was on Cyber Patrol's list of dirty phrase keywords. The list of blocked sites could not be edited, but the list of dirty phrases was viewable and you could add and remove terms from it. Presumably to avoid offending the parents who had to deal with it, the company put in word fragments instead of whole words. The list contained phrases such as "uck" and "ank," the latter apparently an abbreviation for "spanking" because the company wanted to block pages and chat channels about spanking fetishes.

There are many other examples, some involving programs that even remove words from the pages as they download them, without making it obvious that words were removed. Sites blocked by these programs are much more controversial, because the company can control exactly what is on the list. If you find something that is blocked, then they cannot claim they did not know in advance. Supposedly, everything on the list was checked for accuracy in advance.

We periodically do reports, published on the Peacefire.org site, about what types of sites we have found blocked. We focus on sites blocked by the list-based programs; finding sites blocked by the keyword-based programs is not very interesting, because you almost always find some part of almost every site blocked by something like CYBERSitter. If someone wants to know if they have standing to challenge a local library filtering ordinance, and they want an example, I say: "Well, if you have 20 or more documents, I will just run it through CYBERSitter and one of them will be filtered."

The main controversy regarding list-based programs is how they create the list of sites to block. The lists are divided into categories. If a site is classified into one of these categories, then the site will become inaccessible. This gives the illusion of more flexibility than really exists. If you are using, say, SurfWatch and you elect to block only sex sites, then you block sites that SurfWatch has classified under its sex category, which may or may not be accurate. Even if it were accurate, it might not agree with your views on what a sex site is. Even if you did agree with the company on what qualified as a pornography site, the actual review process might not be accurate.

7.3 EXPERIMENTS BY PEACEFIRE.ORG

We are one of the third parties that designed experiments to test the accuracy of the lists used by these companies. There are a couple of ways to do this. The list of blocked sites is supposed to be secret and is not published, but it is always stored in a file that comes with the software. A client-based program has a local list, and periodically you update the list by downloading the latest version from the company that makes it. You can try to break the code on the file and decrypt it, using either Unsoftware or something else. I wrote a decryption program for CYBERSitter in 1997, and two other programmers wrote a decoding program for Cyber Patrol in 2000. You run one of these programs on a computer that has CYBERSitter or Cyber Patrol installed, and it reads the file, decrypts it, and prints out the list of blocked sites into a text file.

The Digital Millennium Copyright Act (P.L. 105-304) was passed in 1998. The Library of Congress was designated to set out regulations for how parts of that act would be enforced. Part of the act prohibited decryption of certain files perceived to be storing trade secrets of the company that produced them. The Library of Congress, which had been following the controversy regarding third parties decrypting lists of sites blocked by blocking software and criticizing them, specifically said that the act of decrypting the list of sites blocked by a blocking program would be considered exempt from this law. But at the time these programs came out, there was no such exemption, so many people were worried about the consequences.

If you have a server product installed on the Internet service provider's system, then you do not have access to the file where the list of blocked sites is stored. In that case you need to do a traffic analysis instead of decrypting. The hard way is trial and error, looking at your favorite sites in a directory like Yahoo. The easier approach is to run a list of sites through the program. I have written scripts that run a large number of URLs through one of these programs and record exactly which ones are blocked. This takes some programming skill, and third parties who review this type of software generally do not go to this much trouble. Reviewers for *Consumer Reports* or *PC Magazine* usually just use the trial and error approach. The flaw in that approach is that if you want a small sample of sites and you get them from a place like Yahoo—perhaps sites in one of Yahoo's pornography categories—then you will get an overly good impression of the software, because the software gets its list of pornography sites from the same type of place. Any good program should block 100 percent of those sites. You want to test a larger sample of sites to get a more reliable accuracy rate.

In one study, we took a cross section of 1,000 dot-com domain names from the files of Network Solutions, which keeps track of all 22 million (and counting) dot-com sites. We wanted to do a random selection. The problem was that if the blocking error rate came out too high with a random selection, then anyone could claim that we stacked the deck by not taking a really random sample. This is a deeply politicized issue, and the companies knew me as someone who had strong feelings about it. It would be too easy for them to say that we must have cheated by using a disproportionate number of sites that we knew were errors. Therefore, we took the first 1,000 dot-com sites in an alphabetical list of all of the sites, because the first ones are not any more or less likely to contain errors than the rest of the list. They all began with "A-1," I think.

This report is linked to my subpage. You can see the 1,000 sites that we used and the ones that are blocked and which ones of those we classified as errors or nonerrors. The sites that we classified as inaccurately blocked were cases in which we believed that no reasonable person could possibly believe that they were accurately blocked. These sites were about things like plumbing, aluminum siding, or home repair toolkits. There was absolutely no doubt that these were errors; we did not encounter any borderline cases at all. I did the analysis again using 1,000 random dot-com sites, and, for all cases, it looked like the result was within 10 percent of the error rate we got doing it the alphabetical way.

We publicized this report with a strong caveat that the second digit of the error rate should not necessarily be taken as accurate. For example, if the error (false positive) rate is 50 percent, we are saying that 50 percent is likely to be close to the actual error rate. If a company claims that it is 99 percent accurate, and we get 30 blocked sites and 15 of them are errors, we can determine with almost 100 percent accuracy that their 99 percent figure is false. Our 50 percent figure could indicate an error rate anywhere from 30 percent to 70 percent, but we definitely can say that 99 percent accuracy is a false claim.

Of the 1,000 dot-com sites in the study, programs blocked anywhere from 5 to 51 sites. Of those blocked sites, how many do we feel were errors? In the case of the five blocked sites, the error number is not meaningful. In the case of 50 blocked sites, there is a certain spread of error. The intent was not so much to come up with a hard number for accuracy but rather to address the question of whether the "99 percent" claims are true.

Here is what we found. Cyber Patrol blocked 21 sites, and 17 of them were mistakes. These were not borderline cases at all; these were sites selling tool hardware, home repair kits, and stuff like that.[1] The examples of blocked sites are listed on our page, so you can verify which sites from the first 1,000 were recorded as blocked or not blocked. We took screen capture images of the sites being blocked, showing the message, "This site has been blocked by this software." Obviously, screen capture is not proof, because it is trivial to fake an image. But there is a danger of people

---

[1]Bob Schloss asked whether the same host might be hosting both a pornographic site and a hardware site, and, because of the way in which domain names, IP addresses, and port numbers are mapped, the hardware site ends up blocked along with the pornographic site. Susan Getgood said Cyber Patrol formerly contained a bug that allowed this to happen—which Peacefire.org may have known about and used in designing the test. She said the technical problem involving hosted servers has been solved in all network versions used in schools and libraries. Bennett Haselton noted that the company's Web page specifically said that material does not have to be blocked because it shares an IP address with another blocked site; if it is true that IP address sharing is the cause of blocking, then this is a false claim. The Web hosting issue has been around for several years and also applies to proxy servers. The BESS filtering system and the parental controls of America Online see the host name, not the IP address, of the site that a user tries to access, so they should not have this problem.

being suspicious that the study was done incorrectly, that there was a bug in our scripts to record the number of sites blocked, or maybe a site was down at the time and we mistakenly entered it as being blocked.

A rate of 17 errors out of the first 1,000 dot-com sites on the list extrapolated across the entire name space of 22 million dot-com sites yields a figure of several hundred thousand incorrectly blocked sites in the dot-com name space alone, not even counting dot-org and dot-net name spaces.

SurfWatch's error (i.e., false-positive) rate was 82 percent; it blocked 42 sites incorrectly and 9 correctly. Even though the same company owned SurfWatch and Cyber Patrol by that time, the lists of sites they blocked turned out to be different. AOL's Parental Controls, which supposedly uses Cyber Patrol's list, blocked fewer sites, possibly because it was using an older version or because the list was frozen after they licensed it from Cyber Patrol. When we found the Surf Watch number, we knew that we had better get all the back-up documentation we could possibly get, because there was such a high error rate. The reason that people do not get these high error rates when casually testing the software is that they test their favorite sites or sites that they know about, and errors in popular sites already have been spotted and corrected. They get an overly good picture of how well the software works.

People spend a certain amount of time on sites that everyone else spends time on; however, people also spend time on sites that are less popular. Therefore, we are concerned about errors in the less popular sites, even though we know that the popular sites contain fewer errors. Moreover, the SurfWatch error rate is not okay if you are one of those 42 sites blocked incorrectly. We plan to do a follow-up study in which we look at the error rates in a sample of 1,000 sites returned from a search on Google or Alta Vista, in which the more popular sites are pushed to the top. I expect that the error rate in that sample will be lower, because the popular sites are weighted more heavily.

This study measured only the percentage of blocked sites that are mistakes—false positives. It did not measure the percentage of pornographic sites that are blocked, or the percentage of nonpornographic sites that are not blocked. If we use either of those numbers to judge a program, then we run into a problem. To determine how good the programs are at blocking pornography, we first would have to find out how many of the 1,000 dot-com sites are pornographic and then see how many are blocked.

We used the same 1,000 dot-com sites for every program except BESS (a filter made by N2H2), which blocked 26 of 1,000 sites, 19 appropriately and 7 by mistake. We did the experiment first with SurfWatch, and that one was published first last August. We thought the other companies might have heard about the first study and perhaps fixed their programs to block fewer sites incorrectly in that small 1,000 site sample. It turned out that none of them apparently had heard about it, because their error rates were the same as before—except for BESS. In BESS, we observed a clean break in the error rate pattern. We took the first 2,000 dot-com sites, and the first 1,000 contained no errors; but right after that, the error pattern appeared.[2] Technically, all they did was fix errors in their software, so can we accuse them of cheating or not? They removed errors from the sample that they knew we were using, so we used the second set of 1,000 dot-com sites.

Our conclusion from this study was that the people are not actually checking every site before they put it on a list. If there are 42 errors in the first 1,000 dot-com sites in a list, then there is no way of knowing how many errors will occur throughout the entire space of 22 million. This does not necessarily mean there is a conspiracy at the highest levels in the company. The most innocent explanation may be that some intelligent, lower-level employee whose job it was to find these sites may have written a program that scoured these sites and added them to the list automatically, without the person having necessarily having to look at them first. There is not necessarily an explanation for how someone could have looked at one of these sites and determined that it was offensive.

The borderline cases receive a lot of attention, because someone brings them to the company's attention and they have debates about whether or not the blocking is appropriate. This happened with an animal rights page that was blocked by Cyber Patrol, for example. There was a discussion about whether the depictions of victims of animal testing were appropriate. But the vast majority of blocked sites that have not been viewed are moving targets, because if you raise the issue of these sites, then generally the company will fix the problems right away. Then it becomes a question of finding more blocked sites. That was why we did the study using 1,000 dot-com sites, so that, even if these specific errors were fixed, the fact that we found them in this cross-section says something about the number of errors that exist in the list as a whole.

Sites can be blocked erroneously for reasons other than a lack of human review. In an incident that became the baseline in discussions about the appropriateness of blocking software, *Time* magazine wrote an online article about CYBERSitter's blocking policies and the controversy over

---

[2]David Forsyth suggested that the substantial difference in results between tests of 1,000 sites and tests of 2,000 sites means that 1,000 sites is too small a set with which to conduct an experiment like this.

the blocking of a gay rights advocacy group's Web pages. CYBERSitter put pathfinder.com, *Time* magazine's domain name, on its list. The magazine's Web site has an article written after CYBERSitter blocked the site, which is good, because otherwise nobody would believe me. At the other end of the spectrum, I sent e-mail to Cyber Patrol saying that the American Family Association (AFA) Web site, the home page of an extremely conservative organization, should be blocked as a hate site because of the amount of antigay rhetoric. Because most programs that publish definitions of hate speech include discrimination based on race, gender, or sexual orientation, Cyber Patrol agreed to block the site. It is still on the list today.

This is an example of controversial blocking. Many of Cyber Patrol's customers would not block this type of site themselves. Many filtering companies, in their published definitions of hate speech, have painted themselves into a corner by including discrimination based on race, gender, and sexual orientation. There are many extremely conservative religious organizations, reasonably well respected, that publish speech denigrating people based on sexual orientation. It does not have to be hateful; it just has to meet the discrimination criteria. ("I Hate Rudy Giuliani" is not a hate site.) Even though anti-gay hate speeches generally are considered politically incorrect, it is not so politically incorrect that many people favor blocking it in a school environment, the way they might favor blocking the Ku Klux Klan Web site.

We did an experiment a couple of months ago in which we nominated some pages on Geocities and Tripod to be blocked by SurfWatch, Cyber Patrol, Net Nanny, and some of the other companies, saying that the quotes on the pages constituted antigay hate speech. The quotes said things like, "We believe that homosexuality is evil, unhealthy, and immoral and is disruptive to individuals and societies." The companies agreed to block the pages. Then we said we had created these pages, and they consisted of nothing but quotes taken from the Focus on the Family Web page or the Dr. Laura Web page. We asked the companies if, to be consistent, they also planned to block these sites as well. So far, all the companies have declined to do this. Net Nanny was the only one that responded, saying it would consider blocking the subpages of sites that contained the material that was blocked when copied to the other page. But about 6 months have passed since then, and the company still has not done it.

We concluded that an unspoken criterion for whether or not to block a page is how much clout the organization that owns the page has and whether it could incite a boycott against the filtering company. If Dr. Laura talked on her radio show about how Cyber Patrol or SurfWatch blocked her Web site, this has the potential to alienate a good proportion of potential customers, as well as possibly leading to a situation in which someone sues a local school or library for blocking access to political speech. If conservatives join forces to raise a legal challenge to speech blocked in a school or library, then it becomes a larger problem. Even without that experiment, the point is still valid. The companies say they block speech that is discriminatory based on race, gender, or sexual orientation. Yet we have examples of unblocked sites run by large or well-funded groups that—no reasonable person could disagree—meet that definition.[3]

We recently published two reports about Web sites blocked by various programs. These reports are linked to our main page. One is Blind Ballots, about candidates in the U.S. elections in 2000 whose Web sites were blocked; these candidates included Democrats, Republicans, and one Libertarian, blocked by BESS and Cyber Patrol. The other report is Amnesty Intercepted, about Amnesty International Israel and other human-rights-related Web pages blocked by programs such as SurfWatch, BESS, Cyber Patrol, CYBERSitter, and some of the others.

These reports were published just before the U.S. Congress passed a law requiring schools and libraries to use blocking software if they receive federal funding. I think the reports will still come in handy later as the debate continues about the appropriateness of blocking software. Just because these reports did not stop passage of the law does not mean that they will not be used as evidence in the court cases to be filed regarding the legality of the law.

There is a question about whether some of the more obvious mistakes made by blocking software can be avoided if you disable the function that dynamically examines pages as they are downloaded and blocks them based on certain keywords. If the list of blocked sites was assembled using keyword searches, and if the pages were not necessarily reviewed first, then the keyword blocking cannot be turned off if the software is installed in an environment (such as a library) in which the administrator wants to be extra careful about not blocking sites that should not be blocked.

---

[3]Susan Getgood said that Cyber Patrol reviewed the four pages that Peacefire.org created and blocked them. The company also reviewed the four source sites but decided not to put them on the list. Cyber Patrol does block afa.net and will continue to do so; AFA promotes a boycott of Disney because it offers same-sex partner benefits. Getgood said that Cyber Patrol is not afraid of an organization's clout; she receives mail from the AFA every 2 months asking for a site re-review, which is done. Bennett Haselton said that the AFA is less mainstream than other groups focusing on the family, such as the Family Research Council, which has a large lobbying group in Washington, D.C.

7.4 CIRCUMVENTION OF BLOCKING SOFTWARE

Blocking software can be circumvented. The easiest way is to find pornography that is not blocked. If you run a search, it is not difficult to find unblocked sites. Everyone who runs a search, with small changes in the query, will get a completely different list of results, so you often find at least one site that is not blocked. You also can disable the software, either by moving files around or by running programs to extract the password. I have written some of these programs. I wrote them because the standards that people use to determine what is indecent and pornographic strike me as arbitrary and silly. I have never heard an explanation for why a man's chest, but not a woman's chest, can be shown on TV. The companies that make the software are reinforcing those standards of decency.

Whether parents should have a right to filter is still a political issue. I think that rights are more abstract; it is difficult to talk about them. I wrote these programs because I believe that no harm is done if you see something that your parents do not want you to see. All of us can think of things that our parents did not want us to see when we were growing up. All of us can think of examples of when we thought they were wrong, and some of us still believe that they were wrong.

People would not use a program like this just to find pornography, because it is trivially easier to find pornography than to disable the software. People use such a program if they need to access a specific site that happens to be blocked. This is either a borderline case, like a sex education site, or something that you do not think should be blocked at all. People have asked me whether I think nothing ever should be blocked. I usually give the example that, if I had a friend whom I thought was depressed and likely to read something that might provoke suicide, then I might go out of my way to try and stop him or her from reading that material. What I would not do is say, "If they're under 18, then I have the right to interfere, but if they're over 18, I can't stop them." I think that criterion is arbitrary and silly, and that it's a red herring people use to avoid thinking about the real censorship issues at stake.

Anonymizer.com is a site that enables you to circumvent blocking software. You can connect to a third-party Web site through Anonymizer, which has a policy of not disclosing who is being redirected to connect to a site. Anyone can circumvent blocking software by going to Anonymizer and typing in the site that they want to access, because blocking software looks at the first site you connect to, not the URL. However, all blocking software blocks Anonymizer. We never make a big deal out of this, because it is not something worth complaining about. SafeWeb is a site that does the same type of thing.

Translator services also are blocked. Babelfish.AltaVista.com is a site where you can type in the URL of a foreign language site and the words from that language will be translated to English, or vice versa. The rationale behind blocking this site was that otherwise the pictures would come through. But Babelfish cannot be used to access images because it does not modify the image tags. (The images are loaded from the original location because Babelfish does not want that data traffic.) The text comes through translated (poorly) but the images are blocked. We published a short piece on why this was probably an unnecessary overreaction on the part of the blocking software, because the text is converted and the images are not accessible.

The third example is Akamai.com, a content distribution service. If you sign up, then the images on your site—instead of being loaded from your site—can be loaded through Akamai's server to save on your bandwidth costs. It is a caching service with servers distributed around the country. A person who requests one of these images will get it directly from the server closest to them. It is a complex scheme that can shave seconds off the load time of a page, so many people place a high value on it. The catch is that a loophole in the software allows you to put any URL on the end of the page, and it will fetch the page through Akamai and deliver it to you.[4]

We pointed this out last August, but it still works. Some people knew about it before then; they had just published a page on how to use this technique and how often it works to unblock a blocked site. The problem is that if the blocking software companies were to block it, they also would block many banner ads served by Akamai. It is used mostly for banner ads to save on bandwidth costs. Large sites, such as Yahoo, also use it to serve their own images.

Programs installed on a network are more difficult to circumvent by moving files around or disabling the software locally, but you can circumvent them by finding unblocked pornography or using the Akamai trick. In addition, if you have the cooperation of someone on the outside willing to set up an Anonymizer-type program on a server, then you can go through that program to access whatever you want. This is becoming easier to do, and people are starting to publish smaller and more lightweight versions of Anonymizer that anyone can put on a Web page as a secret source for them and their friends to use to tunnel through and ac-

---

[4]Milo Medin emphasized that this is a bug, which should be fixed, as opposed to a generic issue.

cess blocked sites. We are working on one of those. It does all kinds of fancy things, such as scrambling the text on the source page and using Java script code to unscramble the text and write it. The censoring proxy server cannot block the page unless it parses the Java script to figure out what the actual text is.

To summarize, two points are important. First, a significant percentage of blocked sites have not been reviewed by humans. This situation may be due to honest errors, such as IP address sharing or employees whose eyes are glazing over. But one way or another, significant amounts of content are blocked that should not be. Second, it is easy to circumvent blocking software.

8

Authentication Technologies

Eddie Zeitler

I work in information security and would like to provide a business perspective on the difficult questions this committee is addressing. Security implementations must resolve whether the measures are to protect honest people from honest problems or are to provide ironclad solutions. The answer makes a big difference in what we implement. In addition, we are chasing technology. If I were trying to subvert a secure system, I would wait for the next communications protocol to be implemented or the next revision to the operating system to be installed. We have unlimited opportunities with computer systems to change whatever works today into something that will not work tomorrow.

8.1 THE PROCESS OF IDENTIFICATION

I will approach identification and authentication from the perspective of the individual, that is, how a child or person is identified to a system. We prove who we are in a number of ways, such as with a driver's license, passport, badge, signature, or fingerprint. When I provide an identifier to you (or tell you who I am), that identifier needs to be authenticated. In the computer world, we use something you know (e.g., a password), something you have (e.g., a credit card with a magnetic stripe), or something you are (e.g., a face, a fingerprint, a retinal scan) to authenticate an identity. Note that, usually, my possession of an identifier does not authenticate my identity.

Some authenticators are much more secure than others. We all know and love our four-digit personal identification number (PIN) and password authenticators. However, administrators of multigigabyte or terabyte databases have password authenticators that are necessarily 20 or 30 characters long. The authenticator, whether weak or strong, needs to be verified.[1] This is where we tend to run into trouble. The process of verifying the authenticator requires a trusted source. In the example of a driver's license, we trust the Department of Motor Vehicles (DMV). The picture on your driver's license is the authenticator. To identify a person you look at the picture on the license, you look at the person presenting it, and say, "Yes, I have authenticated that this is your license and I now believe your identity." The reason this works is that I trust the license because I trust the DMV. If we did not trust the DMV licensing process, then we would not use a license for identification.

If you sign something to authenticate yourself, I have to verify that signature against a trusted copy of your signature. The trusted copy I use to verify it against gives me the confidence that you are who you say you are. For example, a bank's trust is based on properly issued signature cards.

A token typically is not a sufficient authenticator by itself because it can be passed around—it is too mobile. But if implanted permanently in someone's head, that token probably would have some validity. If I have a microchip embedded in my skull at birth by a National Security Agency (NSA) surgeon, and the NSA verifies the chip when I walk through magnetic readers, then I would trust it. But I cannot think of anything less draconian that would suffice to make a token a valid independent authenticator (we tend to use them in conjunction with other authenticators such as PINs).

In summary, the ability to identify a person depends on confidence. You have to have confidence in the authenticator, the issuer and issuing process of the authenticator, the source of the information used to verify the authenticator, and the process used to verify the authenticator. A system that identifies millions of people must have very high confidence. For example, in the case of automated teller machine transactions, a very small error rate in identification would make them unacceptable. If you do not have enormous confidence in the identification process, it is not

---

[1] David Forsyth gave the following example: He has a piece of paper given to him by someone trusted that says, "David Forsyth knows the factors of this very long number." He gives someone else that piece of paper and tells the person these factors. In the authentication, that person says, "Well, if you cannot trust the person who gave you the piece of paper, then the whole thing will not work." Eddie Zeitler added that verification means that he knows that the piece of paper actually came from the person from whom Forsyth said it came. He has verified the "signature."

appropriate for use by a large population (including some who may be trying to defeat the system).

8.2 CHALLENGES AND SOLUTIONS

In the digital world today, technology is rarely the problem. Technology is changing so fast that, if a problem is not solved today, then it will be solved next week. Note that the opposite is also true. A technology that is secure today may not be secure tomorrow. Today we have very high confidence in digital signatures based on public key cryptography.[2] The digital signing processes are good. We are able to identify, authenticate, and verify a person and his or her age very easily using digital signatures. However, the authentication and verification processes are problematic. If they really worked, then the banking community, the brokerage community, and the rest of the financial world would have implemented them years ago. We have the technology to create digital signatures that we all trust, but we do not have an infrastructure in place that makes this process workable.

The private key that you use to create your digital signature will be 1,000 to 2,000 characters long. Where will you put it? It has to be stored in an automated device of some sort. To date, smart tokens, or smart cards, are the best answer. Note that if I put my private key in my computer, we would be authenticating the computer, not me. What I want is something that, wherever I am, can be plugged into any machine to identify me. I do not want it to identify the machine, because then others using that machine could also identify themselves as me if they knew how to use the signing software, which, if they have possession of the machine, they can figure out how to do.

If we use cards, there must be universally compatible software, card readers, and signing processors. I have been involved in writing American National Standards Institute (ANSI) standards for banking, and "universally compatible" is more difficult to accomplish than it is to specify in a standard. We rarely achieve it. In software today, the signature process is fairly standard but the interfaces tend to be different.

Another thought is that if I have my secret key in a personal device (smart card), then I can use that secret key to create a signature. To au-

---

[2] A question was raised as to the applicability of zero-knowledge proofs—proving something to someone without revealing anything that you know. But this has not proved to be practical. Some years ago, I (Zeitler) delved into zero-knowledge systems and found out that, at least for the Bank of America, they did not make a lot of sense.

thenticate the person using that card to the signing system, we typically require a PIN (usually four or six digits). Remember, security is only as good as its weakest link. We have sophisticated software, complex technology, and great cryptography, and it all depends on a PIN.

Then we need a trusted authority to verify the digital signature, someone to say, "Yes, that really is Ed Zeitler's signature." Since it is a digital signature, it must be something more than comparing one piece of paper to another piece of paper. You would go to the agency that issued the secret key and ask, "Is this signature based on this person's secret key?" The agency would respond. Note that I have to trust that agency.

If I am the agency giving you a private key to use to create your signature, I had better know to whom I have given it. So far, the only way we have found to accomplish this is in person. That is how you get a driver's license. Banks want some verifiable form of identification from you in their branch office. In the financial world, there are many stipulations that you know your customer. However, in the online world, banks and brokerage firms do not strongly verify the identity of their customers anymore; they have necessarily resorted to less secure verification processes.

A very secure process and database are necessary to assign cryptographic keys. The people who assign those keys had better have them locked up tight and require strong authentication of a person requesting them. A digital signature cannot be created with a four-digit PIN for authentication. If we do not have a lot of trust in this process, it becomes a house of cards that comes apart, regardless of the zippy technology used.

Today we have digital signature software on all browsers, which is great. We were all applauding when that happened. But we still do not have card readers. We do not have a practical way to issue private keys to millions of people or a practical way to store those keys. The NSA and National Institute of Standards and Technology (NIST) have ventured into this area and have not been successful.

We do not have a trusted party to issue cryptographic keys and verify digital signatures at the national level. U.S. government intelligence agencies would not be satisfactory to the private sector. The trusted party does not have to be a government agency, but what other organization has the presence? When we started developing public key cryptography, we talked about the U.S. Postal Service issuing keys. There are also liability issues. For example, if the Post Office managed the keys and a major break-in occurred and the whole country lost the ability to process public keys (or digital signatures), whom would you sue? On the other hand, if it were a private concern, that probably would be the end of that private concern. What type of liability do companies such as Verisign, which issues cryptographic keys to the public, have? They have been addressing this issue for years and are comfortable that they have a workable solution. But I am not comfortable with that, because if Verisign's data centers were to blow up, people would have little recourse.

Despite the security flaws, electronic banking works fairly well. I worked in a retail company as the chief technology officer years ago, and I moved to a bank from there. I was amazed to find that the retail databases and systems had much more security than the banking systems at that time. Interbank wire transfers and the like were done in a rudimentary fashion. Anyone who knew the system could break it or cause damage. But the reality is that there was very little loss. There were reciprocal agreements between banks. If I sent you a $100 million transfer and realize this afternoon that, oops, it was fraudulent, then the receiving bank will give it back, in most cases. In banking, when you get to the top, only a few people are necessary to make a phone call to gain agreement that, "Yes, we'll take care of that." Although real attacks have been made against our systems, if you want to steal a million dollars, it is still much easier to make friends with the branch manager than to figure out how to break into the automated money transfer systems. Security technology has tended to stay a step ahead of what is practical in the world of financial fraud.

To get back to the beginning of this talk, the definition of "good enough" security depends on the problem to be solved—four-digit PINs may be sufficient in many cases. However, for the purpose of this study, limiting the solution to school or public library computers is vastly different from the problem of identifying a 9-year-old using any computer to access the Web. Most of the computers to which children have access probably will not be run by federal, state, or local governments.[3] A strong identification process will be required.

---

[3] Bob Schloss suggested that there are more incentives for people to steal $100 million or to get the right to launch a nuclear weapon than there are for a 9-year-old to use a school computer to see something that his teacher does not want him or her to see. Ordinarily, the school district gives the smart card to the teachers, who use it to set filters. You cannot forge the PIN. But will one kid who is a computer genius write a device driver that he loads into the computer so that it steals the secret number? Milo Medin suggested wryly that he could simply download it from Peacefire.org.

9

Infrastructure for Age Verification

Fred Cotton

My background is predominantly law enforcement, so I come to this issue having tried to clean up the results of many societal problems, and I see what is going on in the streets. I agree with Eddie Zeitler about authentication and verification. You have to watch it work in the real world with driver's licenses. You can book an individual into the county jail and rely on fingerprint information that does not come back to the right person. You will face these problems anytime you try to superimpose authentication of age onto the real world.

9.1 THE REAL WORLD VERSUS THE INTERNET

How, and to what extent, is interaction with a human being needed to validate identity? Who will validate the validator? Who is it that you trust to say who somebody else is? That level of trust does not exist in any level of government these days. What level of confidence is needed for the accuracy of an assertion of age to pass the legal requirements? The law will define that for you. If you foul it up, you will know. Just as with any other problem in society throughout history, the lawyers will solve it. They will find the tort in the problem, find the person or persons responsible for the tort—either directly or vicariously—and then sue their shorts off. The necessary level of confidence will be defined rapidly as soon as the legal community determines that there is money to be made from it.

What infrastructure is needed to support age checks outside the Internet? We have an existing infrastructure for dealing with credit cards, fingerprints, biometrics, chips in your head, and other things that can be used today. But these things are cost prohibitive and not widely disseminated. To have any kind of authentication process, it has to be globally disseminated; otherwise, there is no standardization. The problem is dissemination. Credit cards are great in the United States but not in the middle of Africa and other places around the global Internet where the infrastructure does not exist. In Third World countries that are developing sites that deal with child pornography and child exploitation, implementing online authentication and age verification technologies is a whole different business.

Cops dealing with problems online tell us that the problem is that our laws only extend as far as our borders, and, historically, our ability to regulate or influence things extends only as far as our laws. Our laws are based on how much territory we can hold with a standing army. This has no application on the global Internet. It is a totally new environment—a brave new world. There is little we can do other than talk about it, because nobody owns the Internet and nobody runs it. Nobody has any say over it other than the people who use it. It is truly a democratic society. When the people who use the Internet get tired enough of something, they will do something about it, independent of government.

Has the Internet environment changed the necessary infrastructure? Obviously, we cannot superimpose the existing structure on the Internet, because of its global and nebulous nature. If you are going to validate identification online, then it has to be standardized to some extent. If you are validated through ABC signature company, and I am a retail merchant who subscribes to XYZ but not ABC, does that mean that you do not get to buy from me? This is probably not going to work well, and something will need to be done about standardization.

What are the costs to the user and to the government? Who will maintain the database of validation? This is a huge responsibility, a huge cost, and a huge security risk. If you blow that one, you are guaranteed to get the legal community involved.

How reliable is the technology? It is reliable today, but tomorrow brilliant little Johnny in the class will figure it out. It only takes one little Johnny to figure it out, and then he automates it and gives it to all the others. We have seen this in computer security for years. It does not require much skill to hack. All you have to do is download the tools that somebody who had the skills to write them made available. It is a point and shoot operation.

Other things that we do in the real world in age verification may or may not have application here. A driver's license is an official ID because we have an official government entity. It is well funded and well staffed, and it requires that you show up to prove who you are before you get the token or identification. It is very difficult to do that on the Internet. I can apply for a credit card through the mail, and I call the issuing company to activate it, and no one there ever actually sees my face. But credit card fraud is easy to commit. People just throw those forms in the garbage. I could go through your garbage and pick up those applications, fill them out, put in a change of address, and charge things in your name. This happens daily. Identity theft is huge. Once you are in that particular loop, getting out of it is next to impossible.

Biometric technologies and fingerprint scans are possible, but it is cost prohibitive for both the user and authentication organization at this time. In addition, the initial validation is always a problem with anything that you superimpose here. Tokens are too mobile. We see that with identities now. We have juveniles buying alcohol over the counter with false IDs, which are not difficult to forge.

Historically, law enforcement protection is a three-legged triangle. It involves enforcement, education, and prevention. Of the three, education is probably the cheapest. This is where you get the most bang for the buck. You simply get people to change their ways by telling them that something is not right, and that it is not in their best interests. So far we have not been very successful with things like narcotics. If we could get people to stop wanting children to access pornography on the Internet, then it would go away.

That leaves you with the other two legs of the triangle. Prevention involves giving parents and teachers some tools that they can use to try to stem the flow. The tools will not stop it but will give them some control over their own part of the environment. The third aspect is enforcement. We find the people who are bringing this grief on us and we bring grief on them, or we find the biggest offenders and put their pelts on the fence as a warning to others. Historically, that is what enforcement is about. We get them to the point where they do not know if they will be next, and they keep their heads down. If they all decide to do bad things at once, there is no law enforcement agency in the world that can prevent it. But we can keep them on their toes enough that they will think twice before they do it.

Everything I have talked about so far deals with the Web, the least offensive of the content problems. How does any of this technology affect e-mail or Usenet? The worst offender is Internet relay chat (IRC), when kids are involved in that arena. I train 30 task forces around the country to do nothing but go after online predators, people who will get on an airplane and go find a child for sex. They spend months and months cultivating that situation. You would not believe the astronomical numbers involved. In that type of environment, all of the screening software and age verification do no good. Technology will not solve this particular problem. Right now, the only thing that is having an effect is enforcement. We are at least identifying the offenders and taking them out of circulation as fast as we can—surgically removing them from society by whatever means is currently socially acceptable.

If you could keep kids off e-mail and Internet Relay Chat[1]—that is, if kids accessed the Internet in a way that worked only through the Web, but ported—then it would eliminate access to children for most of these preferential sexual offenders. But you would also eliminate a lot of things that kids use the Internet for; it would be like keeping kids out of the park or off the telephone. IRC has replaced the telephone after school, and that global circle of friends is a strong social draw. For latchkey kids after school, this is their way of communicating nowadays. With Usenet, if they want to surf for porn, then they will find a public news server and pull off whatever they want. Screening does little about that, particularly with all the things that are mislabeled.

9.2 SOLUTIONS

Any successful effort to keep pornography away from children will have to draw from all available solutions; you need a bit of everything to make it work. No one model will be successful by itself, but, when combined, they likely will have some impact. The degree of impact will depend on the social acceptance of this effort in the long run. The available models include the following:

• Age verification and validation is a positive ID model. Before I can get in somewhere, I must prove that I am an adult. This lends itself to the use of tokens, or what I have and what I know. But this leaves us with the problems mentioned earlier concerning who controls that database and who keeps track of that information.

• The supervision model does nothing at the technological level, but rather has parents supervise kids online. If you put your kids online, then you do not throw them into an electronic pool hall without supervision. You move the computer out into the family room; you do not let kids sit in the back room and do these things all by themselves. Unfortunately, the reality is that most parents do not take the time to do this.

• The software model involves the screening software—Net Nanny, Cyber Patrol, and the others. With the false positives and so on, this is

---

[1] Milo Medin said that he could build a system to do this; the question is whether anyone would want such a product.

problematic, but, when combined with the two approaches mentioned above, it may offer some reassurance.

- The law enforcement model says we go out there and increase our presence online, so it keeps the predators' heads down and keeps them from doing what we want to prevent. They will think twice before engaging someone online, for fear that they are engaging me. This keeps them guessing. This is a fear model.
- The intervention model says we identify the people causing the problem and enlist the aid of the cyber-network neighborhood and crime prevention types so that people who see this activity do not ignore it. They step in and do something about it—they report it, and something happens as a result. This works with burglaries and territorial crimes. We have to rely on the community to tell us how things are going.
- The education model involves improving education to the point where people see that something is wrong and change their behavior. When you change the behavior pattern, it no longer will be socially acceptable or tolerated by the majority of society.

We also need to remove roadblocks in law enforcement that severely limit what I can do online. The rules currently applied to online situations were written for telephones, not the Internet. We work within very narrow parameters. For example, a recent case in the Ninth Circuit dealt with a supervisor going onto a password-protected Web page under the auspices of a pilot during a pilot's strike. The Ninth Circuit said that was not right. If I am a law enforcement officer working undercover, what does that mean for me when I try to access a child pornography Web site? They do not think about the ramifications and how it affects our ability to function online.

I cannot just take your computer, go through it, and find out what is on it. I have to write a search warrant, convince a judge that I have probable cause to believe that what I seek will be there, and show proof of that before someone will give me a search warrant. This is wise, of course. We have these protocols and procedures because you do not want us running amuck and grabbing everything. However, at some point you have to remove some roadblocks if we are to address new technologies based on laws for old technology. We have to remove some of roadblocks so that we can become effective; but we also have to keep parameters in place to keep it from getting out of hand. There is a balance.

The roadblocks have not been collected and presented in an article or publication. They are buried in case law—not even codified law. They are buried in the decisions of the U.S. Supreme Court, district courts, and courts of appeal, in a variety of cases, and in civil lawsuits.[2] Agencies are less concerned about protecting you as a citizen than about getting sued. But we have advocates for change. The U.S. Department of Justice has the tools to do that.

The first thing I would do is to protect children online. We have to find the most egregious cases out there of the providers. I would identify who is causing the problem. Second, if I cannot arrest that person for a violation of law, then I would sic a whole battery of attorneys and law firms on them for a tort violation, basically a violation of my rights. At some point, they will get a clue that this is not acceptable behavior. All of this has to be done within the parameters of the law, but the people causing this problem have to fix the problem. They are causing a problem for the rest of society and they will have to own up to their part and face the consequences.

Criminal prosecution is generally the least effective approach. Using the law is always available; the pen is mightier than the mouth. But the bottom line is, you need to change behaviors. There is no law west of the modem. Look at the development and rapid growth of the Internet, and compare it to the westward expansion of this country in the early 1800s. The same type of thing is happening.

Behavioral changes will be required on both sides. It will require different behavior on the part of people being victimized now. They need to realize that they cannot continue to do these things online without the potential of being a victim. The other behavior we have to change is that of people who look at the Internet as the wild and woolly west, who do not care what they do to anyone else online. You have to change the behavior of children who use the Internet at some point and, by default, change their parents' behavior. I am not picking on any one group. Society as a whole will have to look at this problem and say, "Do we really want this to continue?"[3]

The group causing the biggest problem right now are the offenders,

---

[2]Dick Thornburgh said that someone should read all the cases, collect them, and develop a strong argument for a remedy.

[3]Eddie Zeitler said that, as long as society keeps developing new technologies, these problems will arise. A problem is created when someone puts digitized music in a file and then says you cannot copy it. You cannot commercialize it in the United States, but you can go somewhere else where there is no law against this. No one can tell you that you cannot make copies, because you can, and no one can tell you that you cannot use the Internet, because you can. Fred Cotton noted that, if you send a picture of women without veils to Saudi Arabia, you have sent pornography. In other words, there is also a nebulous community standards issue.

the ones sending material to kids unsolicited, targeting kids, going after them in a planned and concerted manner. That is the first behavior to be changed. They need to wise up and realize that this is not appropriate or face the consequences, because what they are doing is a violation of the law. Sending 12- or 13-year-old kids horrific graphic images is unacceptable to me because the kids do not get a choice. If you tell them, "Hey, do not go over there, because there is bad stuff," and they stay away, then it is fine. But keep the bad stuff over there.

You cannot dry up the supply by somehow taking the money out of it. The sexual predator is not motivated by money but rather by access to children. This cannot be managed like the banking model, in which a concerted effort is made in multiple areas that largely prevents a problem. There are few predators within the banking community, and we tend to get our wagons in a circle when under attack—we control where money goes electronically. On the Internet, nobody controls the pornography supply. You have a widely dispersed supply and a widely dispersed demand, with no central point at which you can install controls.

9.3 THE EXTENT OF THE PROBLEM

When talking about protecting children online, it makes no difference whether it is protection from a sexual predator or a pornographer,[4] because predators use pornography as a tool to lower the inhibitions of children. I have seen them with cartoons of Homer Simpson and Fred Flintstone, telling little kids, "See, Wilma thinks it's okay." There is no difference; pornography is still being put out there and accessed by children. If children are hooked into it and able to go to another site and feed that paraphilia (i.e., unusual sexual preference), then it simply serves to lower the inhibitions further. (Some sexual preferences are illegal; some are not. Child pornography paraphilia happens to be illegal.)

This is like watching violence on TV; eventually, you get numb to it. Most law enforcement officers see the same thing. Finding a dead body on the street is not horrific to me any longer; I have seen too many of them. To the average citizen, it is absolutely horrific, but I have been desensitized to it over the last 27 years. This is sad to say, but it is true of

---

[4]Marilyn Mason asked whether there are two different, but related, aspects to the pornography issue. On the one hand, there are sexual predators who are trying to make contact with juveniles—the scariest part. On the other hand, there are creators of sexually explicit material who are trying to make a buck by selling it, presumably to adults, but sometimes they solicit children as well.

many people who are exposed, over and over again, to things that society does not wish to deal with. Pornography is one of those things.

Just because someone possesses or distributes child pornography does not necessarily make them a predator. But every single predator whom I have dealt with in my 27 years in law enforcement had child pornography—they possessed it, collected it, and used it to entice someone. Predators also use sexually explicit material that is not illegal. The process does not take place overnight. My investigators work on these cases for months. A predator meets a child in a chat room and becomes a friend—talking about things that they cannot talk about with their parents, lowering their inhibitions. The whole object is to get physical access to the kid. These are the people whom I would go after first, because they are the most dangerous. But there is also a group of them who have set up an industry that supports this paraphilia. When they cannot get access to children, they get access to child pornography, because it is the next best thing.

David Finkelhor[5] put together a study for the Office of Juvenile Justice and Delinquency Prevention, published early this year. It was an empirical study of young teenagers online and their contact with sexual predators. Of young girls in the 14-year-old age range that were online, 90 percent of those interviewed had been contacted with unwanted sexual advances. Several went on to further levels. They were interviewed in control groups, too. The numbers were shocking, amazing.

How much of this is unique to the Internet, and how much is just reflective of society in general? For about the first half of my 27 years, I could count on my hands the number of child sexual abuse cases that I handled. With the advent of the Internet, it has grown exponentially. I handled 10 to 15 cases in 1989, the first year that I realized there was a problem. When we started looking at the agencies dealing with it, everyone thought that they were the only one. A segment of our society has this paraphilia or would like to explore it or act it out. They use the Internet as the mask they hide behind. They can play whatever persona they want online, because there is no validation of who they are.

I think we have had child sexual offenders in our society from the beginning, but they used to have to go to extraordinary measures to get access to children. The Internet has made it easy for them. Those who may never have thought of acting out in the real world now have no com-

---

[5]Finkelhor, of the University of New Hampshire, testified at the committee's first meeting, in July 2000.

punction about doing it on the Internet. It is the borderline cases that are coming out now; this is part of the problem.

There is also a phenomenon called validation. If you are into sexually assaulting children, then you are universally disdained in almost every society in the world. You are the lowest form of bottom feeder; if you go to prison, murderers will kill you because you went after a kid. Therefore, when child sexual offenders have the ability to get together in affinity groups they say, "Oh, I'm not the only one. I thought I was the only one, but there are thousands of me out here. And now we can validate it. We can exchange information about children and target children online. We can find out where they live and go and meet with them. This is a wonderful tool."

Just because they talk to one another does not make them easier to catch. It has made for an interesting enforcement environment, but we still have roadblocks that prevent us from catching them. Their Internet communications are in transit, so, technically, we are using forms of wire intercepts. The law was written for the old days of wiretapping the telephone; it does not apply to an Internet chat room. The courts have not defined this well enough. They have not told us what we can and cannot do as far as this new communications medium. As a result, law enforcement is more concerned about getting sued over these types of things. We have to be careful how we proceed.

But these people are coming out in droves. The numbers are astronomical; I have never seen anything like it, and I see no end to it. Children are at risk. Can the risk be managed? Yes, if we implement a variety of different approaches, not just technology, we may be able to manage or limit that risk. But can we eliminate it? Absolutely not. Can we control the global Internet? Probably not. Can we change how people use the Internet through education, prevention, and enforcement? Probably.

10

Automated Policy Preference Negotiation

Deirdre Mulligan

I worked for a long time on the Platform for Privacy Preferences (P3P), which gives parents some control over the data collection practices at Web sites visited by their children. There are instances in which children disclose information about themselves that can be used to contact and communicate with them. P3P has no application in the context of limiting children's access to pornography and other content that might be considered inappropriate.

P3P is a project of the World Wide Web Consortium (which also developed the Platform for Internet Content Selection (PICS)), which enables Web sites to express privacy practices in a standard format. This means that a Web site can make an extensible mark-up language (XML) statement about how it uses personal data.

The basic functionality of P3P is as follows. Say that a Web site collects information such as name, address, and credit card number for the purchase of goods, or it uses clickstream data (i.e., the data left behind when surfing a Web page) to target or tailor information on the Web site to your interests. On the client site, either through a browser or some plug-in to a browser, P3P allows individuals to set parameters for the types of Web sites their kids can visit based on the site's data collection practices. For example, a child might try to enter a Web site that collects data from children and sells it—which is generally illegal in this country without parental consent, under the Children's Online Privacy Protection Act (COPPA).[1] The browser could be set up either to limit access to Web

---

[1]COPPA, which regulates the collection of personal information from children under age 13, was signed into law in 1998 and went into effect in 2000.

sites that engage in that type of data collection or to supply a prompt, notifying the child that "This Web site collects data that your parents have decided you should not disclose."

Several products incorporating P3P are being developed. Most are browser plug-ins. Microsoft will have some P3P functionality in the next generation of Internet Explorer. As with other Web standards, P3P can be combined with other tools and you can plug in certain things, such as trust symbols. You can envision a digital certificate built as an add-on to a P3P application. But the P3P specification itself deals with data collection, not access to different types of content.

The adoption of P3P had little to do with COPPA. Tim Berners-Lee and I gave the first public presentation on P3P at a Federal Trade Commission (FTC) meeting in 1995, several years before the enactment of COPPA. The technology was not specifically designed to deal with children's privacy issues; rather, it was designed to address the need for Web sites to be up front about how they handle data, and the need to implement, on the client's side, tools for individuals to make informed decisions about the disclosure of personal information without having to read all the fine print. P3P is an effort to use the interactivity of the Web to get around some of the barriers and costs associated with privacy protection in the offline world.

The notion of rating is not part of the P3P specification. There is a standard way of talking in a descriptive fashion, which is different from a normative fashion, about privacy. A P3P statement allows a Web site to make descriptive statements—not that their privacy policy is good, bad, or the best, but simply, "We collect this type of information, and we do this with it." Clearly, someone could build a program that makes a judgment. For example, a Web site could say, "We collect everything that we possibly can about you and sell it to everyone in the world." Someone could develop a tool that says that statement equals a bad privacy policy. That tool, in effect, could make a rating based on the descriptive statements.

In many ways, PICS was an effort to provide the capability to make descriptive statements about content. P3P does not provide anything new or special in that area. But descriptive information is not necessarily what people are looking for in the content context; they are looking for normative judgments about what is appropriate, and this is much more difficult to build into a specification. There are constitutional, cultural, and hegemony reasons that make such decisions suspect. It is not as straightforward or factual as statements about what data are collected and how they are used.

Whether P3P leads to more negotiation and customization of content delivery[2] will depend on the implementations. There are a wide variety of implementation styles, and it is unclear how the products will work. Part of it will be driven by consumer demand. Survey after survey has documented enormous public concern with privacy and a real anxiety about disclosing personal information, because people feel that Web sites are not forthright about what they do with data.

A tool that allows people to gain better knowledge about how the data are used certainly may allow more personalization. Some people will choose personalization because they are comfortable having certain types of data collected; if data collection and the personalization it enables are done with the individual's consent, it will advance privacy protection. If a Web site offers the news or sports scores, you might be comfortable telling it which state or county you live in, or your zip code, because the site provides a service that you think is worthwhile. But today you might be anxious about what the site does with the data. If there were a technical platform that allowed you to know ahead of time that only things you were comfortable with would be done with your data, then certainly it might facilitate personalization. But it would be personalization based on your privacy concerns and your consent to the data collection.

With regard to the truth of a site's privacy statements, the question of bad actors is one that we have in every context. There is nothing about P3P that provides enforcement, but it does provide for some transparency, which could facilitate enforcement. In this country, people who say something in commerce that is designed to inform consumers run the risk of an enforcement action by the FTC or a state attorney general if they fail to do what they've said. In other countries, there are similar laws prohibiting deceptive trade practices, and, in addition, many countries have laws that require businesses to adhere to a set of fair information practices designed to protect privacy. Collaborative filtering—a process that automates the process of "word-of-mouth" recommendations by developing responses to search queries based on the likes and dislikes of others who share interests, buying habits, or another trait with the searcher—is independent of P3P. I have not seen a discussion of its applicability in the privacy area.

---

[2]Bob Schloss gave the hypothetical example of *Sports Illustrated* warning that some of its content shows people in skimpy bathing suits, and a user agent (or client) saying it does not want to see sites like this. *Sports Illustrated* could offer to present a subset of its content honoring the request. But why would the magazine go through such complex programming if only 10 people had user agents that could negotiate? To what extent would there be negotiations in which a site would either collect data or provide a subset of its function without collecting data?

11

Digital Rights Management Technology

John Blumenthal

I am a security architect specializing in digital rights management (DRM) systems. I am engaged now in the music and publishing space, but I have a history of looking at rights management in terms of digital products and messaging, e-mail in particular, dealing with issues such as the unauthorized forwarding of e-mails in the sense of how conversations are considered under copyright law and the ability to abuse conversations. I have both a technological hacker perspective and a policy approach that includes a focus on risk management in terms of how to control content.

11.1 TECHNOLOGY AND POLICY CONSTRAINTS

How do we prevent particular types of content floating around on the Internet from reaching certain classes of users? We would like to implement a technological restriction. How do we implement these controls on contents to contain propagation? The Internet is all about propagation. This question raises not only the issue of viewing but also the issue of ownership and super-distribution or forwarding. On the policy and legal side, can this be implemented in a legal structure once you achieve this "nirvana" of a universal technological solution?

Is this really any different from the MP3 debate? There may be social or psychological issues as to why people consume and propagate this type of content, but fundamentally, to look at the MP3 debate is to stare in the face of the problem. The current crisis in the music industry is that this format, MP3, which compresses and renders audio,[1] is not associated with any type of use controls. Napster posts these files, or references to them, such that users can send and swap the files without any control, effectively undermining the music distribution channel, typically compact disk with read-only memory (CD-ROM). The publishers chose not to encrypt the data on CDs, for cost and other reasons.[2] Music on a CD is stored digitally in a totally unencrypted way, which is why you can make copies to play in your car.

There is no way to control this problem technologically; we can only continue to raise the bar, effectively placing us in the domain of risk management. This is the core problem, which I refer to here as the trusted client security fallacy. I have complete ownership of this device, literally, physically, and in every aspect, when it is on a network. This means that, with the proper tools, I can capture that content no matter what type of controls you place on me. There are people within @stake who are experts in reverse engineering, which allows them to unlock anything that has been encrypted. If we attempt a technological solution, then there will be ways to circumvent it, which then will propagate and become much easier for the masses to use.

I believe that policy drives technology in this problem, simply because technology does not offer a complete solution. The only way to attempt a solution to mitigate risk is to adopt a hybrid approach, mixing technology and policy. Whatever system you come up with in the digital rights space must be sensitive to these policy constraints. You have to distinguish the type of content in attempting to invoke rights on it and control it. This is a fundamental premise of the way a DRM system is designed and applied.[3]

These policy constraints create the archenemy of security and content control—system complexities. There are serious economic consequences for the technology industry in general, because you are imposing on the end user experience. You are disrupting and removing things, such as free use of and access to information, that I have become accustomed to using on the Internet. Decisions regarding how to implement the policy and technology will affect this industry.

---

[1] To render means to convert a format into a human-consumable element—displaying data as images, playing data as sound, or streaming data as video.

[2] Milo Medin pointed out that the music publishers themselves created the unencrypted format in which CDs are published, effectively creating this problem. He said we cannot expect people to use a digital management format that offers them fewer capabilities than the native format in which the material originally was published.

[3] References for DRM and client-side controls can be found at <http://www.intertrust.com>, <http://www.vyou.com>, and <http://www.oracle.com>.

The policy constraints causing these problems are privacy, the First Amendment and free speech, censorship, the legal jurisdiction issue, rating systems (which will become difficult to implement and maintain), copyright and fair use, and compliance and enforcement. These are all difficult issues.

11.2 DESIGNING A SOLUTION TO FIT THE CONSTRAINTS

This is how I would approach designing a system that conforms to the policy constraints. Some of this is very technical. First, we have to design a system to operate across all the consuming applications: chat, e-mail, Web browsers, file transfer protocol, and so on. This is a massive infrastructure. Then, given all of the policy constraints, how can we authenticate age—to determine if a user is 18—and only age without stomping on privacy issues? The only thing that I could come up with is biometric authentication. A biometric approach can detect who you are. I have heard that devices exist that can take a biometric measurement and determine the age of that measurement, but I do not believe it.[4]

The collector of the information is responsible for enforcing the privacy issues. If you are willing to go deeper into the privacy issue and maybe involve so-called trusted third parties, porn sites often perform age authentication through the submission of a credit card number. Thus, if you release some of the constraints, you get more of what you want to achieve. But the problem of hacking is inescapable.[5] Gaining access to porn—something forbidden—is probably one of the most deep-rooted psychological motivations for becoming a hacker in the early stages. Talk to any hacker; if there is lurid content, then they want access to it. Music probably brings them into the same psychological realm.

The bigger issue is, now that you provide access, do you permit propagation? In other words, is the authorized user allowed only to view the content? This issue has more to do with content consumption than con-

---

[4]Herb Lin said that he does not believe this; his 6-year-old daughter just had a bone-age scan, which said she is three-and-a-half. Milo Medin suggested that a blood test probably could determine age. David Forsyth suggested counting the rings in a section of a long bone. Herb Lin noted that, to be useful legally, a biometric would have to change suddenly in a significant way between age 17 years and 364 days and age 18 years and 1 day. Milo Medin countered that a real-world system need not be accurate to within 1 day. Gail Pritchard summed up the problem by saying, "The minute I turn 18, I want access." She noted that there are other means for checking a person's birthday.

[5]David Forsyth pointed out the conundrum of "anything I own, I can attack." In other words, if a parent has an age verification system and a technically creative offspring, then the system is essentially meaningless.

tent access. You want to prevent the propagation of certain types of Internet material. There is a subtle, more hidden issue here. If content is provided to someone who is authorized and authenticated, and it is rendered, then you are heavily into DRM. Should the user be permitted to propagate that material to another party such that it is rendered, in effect, in an uncontrolled fashion? The system needs to consider both consumption and propagation issues to provide a whole solution.

In the system that I am designing, I will install a virtual V-chip. Some of you may be familiar with the V-chip Initiative,[6] which led to many debates and various laws. As of January 2000, new television sets have this capability. There is a twin effort in the V-chip analogy, in which the so-called client side (i.e., the television, desktop) and the publisher side (i.e., the broadcasters) are driven by policy makers not only to implement this bar to maintain risk on the client rendering side, but also to come up with a rating system so that the V-chip can look at a stream of art or video and say whether it is inappropriate content. The parents have set up this virtual ratings wall to prevent the rendering of, and access to, the content.

As applied to television, the V-chip impedes the user experience so onerously that people do not use it. Instead, they police the use of television by simply physically being in their children's presence—or they do not police it at all.[7] A lot of work would need to be done with both the

---

[6]See <http://www.cep.org/vchip.html>, <http://www.fcc.gov/vchip.html>, <http://www.webkeys.com>.

[7]Janet Schofield said that parents typically do not police their children's television use systematically. Linda Hodge said that parents do not trust the filtering system because the broadcasters themselves set V-chip ratings, which are voluntary, and they have no incentive to use them. Janet Schofield said that many parents do not believe that the violence seen on television is really a problem, at least not to the degree that they don't watch things they want to see because their children will be exposed to it. When she talks to kids about experiments on the connection between television violence and kids' behavior, she loses their interest. She said parents or adults would take pornography issues more seriously than they do violence, so there may be a difference in motivation to use the filter. Sandra Calvert noted that the V-chip is not designed to censor violence only; it also screens sex and language. It has about five different ratings: fantasy violence, real violence, sex, language, and so on. Robin Raskin said parents are not using filters on their PCs or AOL's parental controls either, because they do not see the link between entertainment and behavior. Part of the problem is that the research on this link is 20 years old and not very good. Sandra Calvert said that people who watch violence but are not incited to kill by it tend to disbelieve the general findings in the literature about the connection, which depends on the individual. But there is a new review article showing a link between playing aggressive video games and being aggressive personally, for both males and females. People can become desensitized to violence and no longer pay attention to it. At this time, the culture is not so desensitized to pornography, but this could become a problem.

purveyors of this technology (Microsoft and Intel) and the publishers on the server side offering up the content. The complexity and impossibility of this problem starts to avalanche here.

A precedent to frame thinking in this debate is encased in an interesting act of 1990 that ultimately led to this technology. The first initiative to look at is the Platform for Privacy Preferences (P3P).[8] I argue that extensions to this initiative, in effect, could implement a rating system. This would be done using the extensible mark-up language (XML), a revolution in the industry and the treatment of content. XML is a natural evolution from HTML.[9] It provides more power and will be the native format in which all Microsoft documents are stored. (Today, Word is stored in a format proprietary to Microsoft.) The XML processing engines sit inside the operating system, at least in forthcoming versions of Windows; virtually every device in the world will be capable of parsing that type of content. The idea is to modify the processing engine to require a P3P rating. If the description of the P3P rating is not in the content, the processing engine will not render it. This would force everyone in the industry to adopt this standard on a global basis.

This idea is not that farfetched. HTML achieved global status over a period of time; XML will achieve similar status over a period of time. XML already is being applied in various ways that have a global effect. The idea of modifying client applications that already use the underlying XML processing engine is not a stretch either. XML even could be extended to handle commerce material (e.g., from Napster). This initiative, which is in front of the World Wide Web Consortium, is achieving standards that are unprecedented. P3P is not a burdensome implementation, either, technologically. It is in line with where the vendors are going with a whole slew of other initiatives.

Next, you would need to start applying pressure on software industry giants and possibly hardware industry giants, too. In doing so, the entire client-side security fallacy—that you can control the rendering of content on an untrusted and unsecured host—must be recognized. The only way to compensate for it is through policy, by going after the people who create compromises in reverse engineering of the system itself. The

---

[8]See <http://www.w3c.org/P3P>.

[9]Nick Belkin said that, so far, XML has done only what HTTP has done—formal characterization. No one has had any significant experience with content characterization. If this is done, then a database is needed that incorporates ontology that describes the whole thing, and someone has to construct and maintain the database. Bob Schloss said there would be an announcement soon related to this issue by a consortium of companies.

Digital Millennium Copyright Act of 1998 outlaws some of these techniques. It did not stop the DeCSS[10] model, but it did end up in court.

Reverse-engineering techniques would permit me to create controls around the content of any type of system. Reverse engineering unleashes content across all of computing. It is one of those difficult problems that have not been solved in the computer science field. Embedded systems raise the bar,[11] but you create a cottage industry of reverse engineers who will get down to assembly level code and remove the actual execution set on the chip and replace it. This is done widely now. There are ways of raising the bar continually;[12] the question is, how far you want to raise the bar and, in doing so, affect the industry in many different ways.

If we implement such a solution in the turbulent waters of the industry now, we would create an interesting and difficult problem. Some giants, such as Microsoft, want to dominate the content-rendering space, and whoever wins that battle effectively dominates digital entertainment. Microsoft is the best positioned to do this, as America Online and everyone else knows. The interesting economic and political issue is that the operating system vendor would dominate this area. If this solution were implemented in the interests of policy, then the vendors would scramble

---

[10]DeCSS is software that breaks the Content Scrambling System (CSS), which is weak encryption used for movies on digital versatile disks (DVDs).

[11]Herb Lin said it would be very difficult, although not impossible, to do on-screen decryption. In principle, you could build into the display processor some hardware that decrypts data on the fly before they are put on the screen. Milo Medin noted that such technology is used for high-definition television. David Forsyth said the problem with raising the bar is that you only raise it for one person. The federal courts say that DeCSS is naughty, but he has DVDs stolen from a Macintosh that required no programming to obtain.

[12]Milo Medin said the problem with standards is that computer power increases. A DVD player cannot send out raw, high-depth material; it has to be encoded in some way. (A PC does not have this constraint.) This requirement is in the license signature process for DVDs. All consumer devices have the same fundamental issue. You want to build a standard that consumer electronics companies can blast into hardware, make cheap, and make widely available. You want that standard to last for 10 to 20 years. To make an affordable device when the standard is released, there must be a manageable level of complexity and security. But 10 years later, a computer is much faster, and the standard cannot change. Anything that uses a fixed standard for cryptography is doomed. DirecTV dealt with this problem in the right way. People often steal the modules and clone them. One Superbowl Sunday, the company turned off about half a million to 1 million pirate boxes. Over time, the company sent down little snippets of code and then, all at once, decrypted the code and ran it, and it changed the way the bits are understood. A flexible crypto scheme is the only way to address this problem. However, it is very difficult to implement in consumer electronics when you do not have a data link; it may be easier in the future when everything is Internet connected.

to provide a solution, not so much to solve this very ugly problem,[13] but rather to control the rendering of music, documents, and images.

Of course, the client security fallacy continues to hold.[14] Once someone has developed a way to circumvent the system, he or she can package it into an application or executable and put it on the Internet, and anyone else who wants to shut the whole system off just clicks on this application.[15] The goal is to raise the bar to a level of hassle so high that only a very motivated individual would engage in cracking it. Such safeguards are all hardware related.[16] Any solution not hardware related will end up with a one-click compromise. When you have to crack open a device

---

[13]Milo Medin said many stupid ideas are circulating in this space. One idea is to put controls in the logic of hard drives so that they will not store or play back files. But as long as the industry wants a cheap, easy-to-display, and easy-to-implement consumer electronics standard, security will remain elusive, because you cannot have all these things and security too. This is a problem that the industry has made for itself.

[14]Milo Medin noted that, as long as a general-purpose operating system is used, someone can circumvent the system by changing a device driver. In fact, a network makes such changes automatically. As long as people can make a change between the XML rendering engine and the underlying hardware, they can get around anything. Dan Geer said another future trend is automatic updating by manufacturers on a regular basis. This is done for two reasons: to ease the burden of updating on the average user, and to handle security problems that cannot wait for system updates. The question of whether the software will run on a desktop internally and belong to the user, or whether there has to be an opening for others elsewhere to reach in and change it as part of a contract or lease, is outside the scope of the present discussion. Herb Lin noted that automatic updates already are made to Norton AntiVirus, Word, and Windows. Milo Medin emphasized that both the software programs and users can do automatic updates. A provider can trigger an update on the desktop of a subscriber at home—a capability built into the software. But the provider cannot prevent the user from also doing an update.

[15]John Rabun said this would be a problem for law enforcement, because many pedophiles would get the chip needed to circumvent the system. However, the system would prevent normal exposure of children to pornography. Milo Medin disagreed. Unless the industry changes the architecture of PCs completely, there will be a way to intervene in instructions by loading executables into an operating system and running them between the hardware and renderer. By contrast, a cell phone is an intelligent device running software that is relatively secure. People cannot make calls with someone else's cell phone because they cannot download programs into it. In the case of the cable modem, the network operator, not the user, controls the code. The problem with PCs is that the user controls the code, and the operating system does not have trusted segments that interplay with the hardware to prevent circumvention. The situation is different with a set-top box, because the operating system is embedded and is managed and downloaded remotely. A user cannot get around it because there is no hook to execute.

[16]David Forsyth gave the example of region codes in the DVD world. If someone wanted to convert a DVD player into a non-region-coded player, he or she would have to fiddle around in the guts of the device. Clear instructions can be obtained from the Internet on how to do this, but most people are inhibited from changing the firmware on their DVD players.

case and replace a chip or do something else that involves hardware, you raise the bar pretty significantly. But this is a general-purpose computer, and the idea of shipping a chip associated with digital rights, which Intel tried to do, has not worked.[17]

I am creating a futuristic scenario, drawing on themes in the industry and technology that are moving toward what I am describing. The older systems that remain in legacy states would not be able to participate in the system; they would not be able to render content as easily as newer systems. The king holding all the cards is Microsoft, because it is the one entity that can modify the operating system to require tags on content for rendering. If Microsoft took that step, then, in effect, you would drive the pressure back to the publishers, who are saying, "If I don't rate, then I don't render." Microsoft can drive this issue, but this brings you back full circle to the question of whether you give it the power to do that.

Let us fantasize about this world in which content is legislated and rated, effectively much like the V-chip. The whole argument over ratings already has been conducted on Capitol Hill, so you would end up with an interesting and difficult technological problem. How do I know that content is accurately rated and that my P3P profile on my browser renders that? How do I enforce the association between the content being posted and the rating that it is purported to have?[18]

There would need to be a law that defines the answers. Technology is part of the solution, but this is difficult technologically. A crawler or piece of software could wander around the Internet, looking at your P3P rating and then descending into your Web site to determine what that content really is and whether it is accurately rated. This is feasible, and it is probably an interesting project for some of the best computer scientists in this country. There are things like this on the Internet today, not necessarily looking at porn, but providing other search engine capabilities. This technology will improve over time. You would have to build a component that is highly complex and globally capable of crawling around the Internet.

---

[17]Milo Medin said Intel would still fail if it tried this approach again today, because people do not want someone else controlling their computers. Robin Raskin argued that it is a trade-off between service and privacy; if Intel can make the users' lives easier, then users will comply. Milo Medin said the problem is that consumer electronic companies want to build cheap devices without elaborate internal workings. All it takes is for one or two people to crack the code and post it to Usenet, and it will be replicated all over the place. Providing access to the content (as opposed to the algorithm) is illegal because of copyright.

[18]Milo Medin said this is a Federal Trade Commission (FTC) issue. There must be a negative consequence for rating aberrations to change behavior. In the privacy arena, everyone posted something in the deal with the FTC, and the FTC said it would pursue anyone who violated the agreement. Bob Schloss suggested a default rating, so that if actual rating information is absent, the content is assumed to be X rated and for adults only.

Realistically, to achieve this system, you would go after Microsoft based on its market dominance in the rendering device itself. If you control that, then you effectively control how things get published to those devices. This would be the creation of a V-chip-like initiative that goes to the heart of a much more homogeneous environment than what the V-chip vendors were concerned about. Technologically, it fits with the P3P protocol and borrows from classification models, such as Label Security implemented by Oracle 9i, that define data and how the rendering client should treat them. But it is still futuristic and requires huge global change. Another layer you can add is policy-based filtering in the network itself. The only way you can approach this problem holistically is with a model that layers additional components of control from the network to the client application and operating system to the publisher.

The publishers will oppose this because it will limit their market reach. Yet they have an incentive to protect copyrights and to have a control model in place. They are all trembling in the wake of the Napster crisis. This is why I hold out hope that solving this problem also solves some of those issues for them.

11.3 PROTECTING CHILDREN

I say it is up to the parent to define a child's user profile during the installation of an application. Many applications do this today: AOL accounts, Netscape, and Internet Explorer offer a profiled login. This way, when a child sits down to use that computer, he or she is constrained by the user profile, which technically becomes intertwined with the P3P profile. Once the child gets past a profile login, his or her Internet world is constrained by the definition of that profile.

This is in line with how you operate today. The difference is that the content you would access in my system would be controlled by the definition of your profile. This link is not strong today; there are no preset rules as to what renders in a browser. I am suggesting that you have to deal with the login issue to gain access to a profile based on your age. This comes back to the question of how you authenticate just age without violating other policy constraints and privacy and so forth. The P3P negotiation occurs at the machine level. For the level of detail in the profile, imagine a sliding bar representing content acceptable to the parent.[19]

---

[19]Robin Raskin said the more granular the P3P negotiation, the less it will be used. Systems do not work when they ask parents to make distinctions among, for example, full frontal nudity, partial nudity, and half-revealed nudity; in such cases, parents decide to let their kids see everything. A good profile requires a lot of granularity, but to convince a parent to use it, it cannot have any nuances.

The privacy issue arises not when a person provides access to personal information but rather when someone else records it. If you focus on the client side, then at least you can throw to the privacy advocates a bone that says, "All of that information is stored locally." But there are systems in which you need a connection to a remote server, and your private information—like a credit card number or some other authenticating token—goes somewhere else. Once you do that, the privacy advocates will descend on this like vultures and pick it apart.

The adult entertainment industry's age verification services move the issue of trust somewhere else. When you give your age, you get a challenge response asking you to prove your age by filling out a form. You might do that with a credit card number or other personal information. You repose this information with the trusted third party. This information could be loaded to say, "Your P3P profile now permits you to see this type of material." But because you send your private information somewhere else, this age verification service, over time, now becomes a list of names of people who want access to porn.[20] You can see the privacy people going crazy about the fact that this database is being used for that purpose.

There is another industry trend that relates to age verification. Dan Geer is probably one of the world's leading experts on this, because he designed the system that Wall Street uses, Identrus, which issues digital certificates to own identity. The forms that describe the identities in those certificates have an age field. There are initiatives concerning the issuance of multiple certificates based on multiple types of identities and use of identity. There is talk in various committees in front of the Internet Engineering Task Force about the issuance of age-specific certificates.

To obtain an age-specific certificate, you would prove to VeriSign that you were born on the following date and your Social Security number is x. Then you can be issued a certificate to be loaded onto your computer. There is discussion in the public key infrastructure community that VeriSign might fill the trusted third-party role, in which it would gain no further knowledge about you other than your age. VeriSign has a bunker that enforces the limits in physical and legalistic ways. I would feel comfortable proving my age to VeriSign, knowing that it is legally bound. In

---

[20]Herb Lin noted that whoever is verifying the age information does not have to keep a list, even though it would be valuable. If people could be sure that no list was being kept, then the privacy issue would disappear. The difference between cyberspace and the real world is that, if a person goes into an adult bookstore and shows a driver's license as proof of age, then the clerk just looks at it and says, "OK." The clerk does not make a photocopy of it and file it away.

fact, VeriSign exists on a foundation of trust that is assumed when you use and obtain its certificates.

This system might indeed provide the trusted third party for age authentication, and it fits with the public key infrastructure. The problem—and Simpson Garfinkel and others have pointed to this in the privacy debates—lies in the meta-aggregation that will come in the future. I will get that database; VeriSign sells data like that. I also will get the clickstream from all the porn sites, and interesting data mining techniques will be used to aggregate and combine these data to trace it back to me and say, "You were the person who did this." There is widespread compromise on the server side—look at Egghead and CD Now. This is an uncontainable problem that you do not encounter until after the compromise has occurred.[21]

11.4 SUMMARY

There are many threats to the system I just designed.[22] Compliance is a major issue, which the search engine industry is addressing to some extent. Bots will be required to crawl the Internet for server-side ratings implementation; anti-bots can be created to defeat compliance checking. Client-side Trojans, worms, and viruses all can be injected into this machine to modify the XML processor. If it has memory, then I can hack it. If it has a processor, then good reverse engineers can create a one-click compromise. Ratings can be stripped off of content, or interesting techniques can be used to create content that appears G-rated to the rendering engine but is actually X-rated. In the Secure Digital Music Initiative, they tried to watermark the content to control it; this was hacked within days. The same thing would happen here. Finally, you would face widespread dissemination of a one-click compromise created by one hacker. "Script kitties" enable people to click on an attack that someone else created to automate everything I described. The scenario is not very hopeful.

---

[21]David Forsyth said you could prohibit people from possessing certain types of data or using them in certain ways. You also could punish violators. But the chances of actually catching them might be very small. Someone could keep a database in a way such that it would be difficult to find.

[22]Herb Lin summarized the presentation as follows: To control distribution of content to only age-appropriate people, you would have to make many changes in the existing technology and policy infrastructure, going far beyond the issue of age verification for inappropriate content. This would offer some benefits but would not necessarily solve the problem.

12

A Trusted Third Party in Digital Rights Management

David Maher

I designed the secure telephone unit that first used the infamous Clipper chip—which further illustrated, to me, many of the issues involved with trusted third parties. I agree that there are major problems with trying to control what people do on their open-system PCs. But we should not give up just because we cannot design a perfect system to prevent a hacker from hacking PCs. There are techniques that can make hacking difficult, and in particular techniques that can allow business models to be supported in spite of security breakdowns. When I saw CSS several years ago, my colleagues and I in the secure systems world shook our heads and said, "As soon as it's rolled out, it (the crack) will be on a T-shirt." In fact, it was. But bad security design does not have to be the rule.

I agree that a lot of infrastructure will have to be rolled out to take advantage of some of the methods and techniques discussed here at these meetings, and many things will have to change. We will become more oriented to digital rights and responsibilities and policies. There will be motivation to roll out some of these techniques, methods, and standards, not only because of digital rights management for the control of copyrighted material in the media and entertainment industry, but also practically for asset management (in enterprises), where some of the challenges are not quite the same. There is a lot of movement and demand to set up the infrastructure for policy and control of the deployment of assets, both within an enterprise and among enterprises.

The context for digital rights management (DRM) has a lot to do with commerce automation, where you have a publisher who wants to publish information, which could be entertainment, pricing information, or a contract, and the publisher wants to give access to the right people, who are allowed to exercise the provisions of the contract. Just about any piece of information that has some value that someone can exercise some right with regard to is the type of thing that you want to be able to control in this sort of system.

12.1 INTERTRUST TECHNOLOGIES

At InterTrust Technologies, we give the publishers tools that allow them to place the content in a container that provides any type of protection that the publisher wants. It can be encrypted or not; it can have integrity protection or not. There could be rules associated with the information placed in the container. There also could be other containers linked to that first container that contain additional rules, such as rules that the publisher thought of later on or rules that say that the previous rules are revoked.

Then you go through a distribution chain, which may have several tiers. According to the rules, people can do various things. They could change the unit price of an object that has commercial value, for example, or they could decide that you can forward it to someone else. Just about any action can be controlled at any level of the distribution chain.

Eventually, however, these things get back to the consumer. In our space, the consumer has to agree to rules, either implicitly or en masse. For example, if there is a license associated with something, then the user must agree to the license, which may make an implicit agreement for many other transactions that might happen down the road. But somehow or other, the consumer must be informed about the rules associated with the things that impinge on the consumer.

As an example, a rule might say that an audit record will be created if you engage in a specific transaction—an audit record that itself becomes protected content. This is done in a way such that the consumer is told, "You can have this piece of content for free. We will collect some unlinked, anonymous information about it, but we need to aggregate that information with information from other people."

InterTrust's role is to ensure that such things are done in a fair and accurate manner. For example, if someone says, "I will not collect data for an audit record about your use of this," we can tell whether that statement is true, because we designed many of the mechanisms. The rules say that if an audit record is supposed to be created but instead an anomaly occurs, then the transaction will not go through. The idea is to have automation not just within the Web, but within any local area networks or personal area networks, such that the consumer could, for example, have some of this content moved into various other types of devices.

Thus, the commerce network—at least in the way that we represent DRM—contains just about any type of digital information. There are also loosely coupled rules, meaning the rules do not have to be packed with the information in the same file. The file can be delivered in one space and the rules delivered in another. In addition, the rules can change; they can expire and things of that sort.

Another important concept is identity attributes, which are applied to principals who may use the information. Rules can refer to those identity attributes. There is a coding system for identity attributes, and a trust management system for determining which identity attributes are associated with what. The identity attributes also could be associated with pieces of information. For example, a rule might say that if you are a Book of the Month Club member, you get a 25 percent discount. There also has to be something, such as labels, that identifies Book of the Month Club selections. These labels are identity attributes in that space.

Events and consequences are an essential part of the DRM system. The content owner identifies the events; for example, if you want to play this particular game, then you have to pay for it. In such cases, content owners might want to see proof of authorization or payment, or they might prefer to say that a meter in some device is decremented or incremented. Or they may want to have, anonymously or explicitly, the identity-linked information or a record of what happened. Some of these events and consequences are practical. In the medical information arena, for example, people are resistant to hard-coded policies on access to medical records, because in emergency situations these policies would not be appropriate.

Therefore, you need exception mechanisms, which are difficult to implement. The exception mechanism might say, "You can have emergency access if you say who you are; then an audit record will be collected and will flow upstream to a clearinghouse, and later on someone may ask you why you did this." At least this approach tends to ensure that the exception mechanism is not abused. Such a mechanism could be useful in the context of labeling content so that children can have access to something on which they are doing a report, even though something like P3P or some browsing policy enforcement software, or whatever, otherwise would deny them access. Creating an audit record is problematical, but at least the parent can say, "I understand that you exercise that exception in a fairly straightforward way and I am still monitoring what you are doing in absentia." When these techniques are applied, the recording of events, logging, and especially exception mechanisms are absolutely required.

An audit mechanism can be defeated by an attack on the communication between the auditor and desktop. The mechanism that we use assumes that you are not always online (most people are not). We can tell whether or not people tamper with the protected database, up to certain limits. There are thresholds that say, "I must deliver my cache of audit records to wherever their destination is." The audit server could be part of an enterprise, or you could contract with an ISP to host the clearinghouse for the audit records. Or it could be part of a home network or part of the same machine such that the parent has access to the audit records but the children do not. It is difficult to implement but conceptually straightforward.

We have a network of protected processing environments. We work directly with chipmakers—such as Texas Instruments, and chip platform makers, such as ARM, and other companies making chips that go in set-top boxes, cell phones, or personal digital assistants—to put in security mechanisms (e.g., trust management) so that we can have a protected processing environment. This is highly problematic for a PC, as observed by others earlier. The mechanisms that we use for the PC are quite different; they have to do with the concept of renewability, also alluded to earlier.

Trust management, or delegation of trust, involves who and what are trusted to do what, and who determines policy. This has do with, for example, those things you delegate to a parent versus a child, and how you arrange the user interface so that people actually understand the policy on what might be delegated to them—a difficult problem in this space. A couple of years ago, AT&T Labs did a demonstration of P3P policy with a user interface, which I thought was the most crucial aspect of the research done at AT&T labs on P3P. A user interface is how you make all of this material understandable. They made a few policies visible. But these were not granular policies, which are difficult to make people understand. Straightforward policies might be difficult to change on a daily basis, but they can at least be tuned, perhaps when installed, using a somewhat more complicated user interface.

There is also the distribution of policies and rules, which can be broken up into three areas of intent: what you want to do with the content, under what conditions you are allowed to do those things, and what the consequences are. Another important concept is action inquiries, that state the conditions under which I even ask the question, "Am I allowed to do this?" There is also governance of transactions, the overseer that ensures that a transaction is carried out. When the answer to an action inquiry is, "Yes, this is allowed, but . . . ," then often it is allowed if you pay or if an audit record is created or whatever. This is the concept of a transaction.

Concurrent events either all occur or do not occur together. There are two-phase approaches to ensuring that governance is enforced that are part of the DRM system but distinct from the trust management system.

12.2 COUNTERMEASURES AND HACKERS

Another part of DRM is renewability, which I think is key to trying to defeat someone who is determined to circumvent the system. I have been involved in the design of protection for satellite entertainment systems, and the sophistication of attacks on these systems might astound some people. One of the best books on defeating these systems is *The Black Book*, which has a skeleton and crossbones on the cover. You can order it on the Internet and it is freely available, published by a charming Irishman named John McCormac. It is humorous, but it also has a lot of code and diagrams of how to defeat various satellite receivers. He also publishes a Web site, the Hack Watch News (at <http://www.iol.ie/~kooltek/>), which has been up for years and is probably still there. At one time this site was filled with hacks and boasts of hacks, but now the hacking is uninteresting, and the hackers seem to be having far less fun.

A number of these satellite systems—the predecessors of DirecTV, for example—were mercilessly attacked. I asked them how they designed systems that could be attacked so easily. The answer was something like the following: "Our contract with the service provider just says to keep the pirates' success rate below a certain level." This is all they really needed to do. More aggressive approaches were either more expensive or more intrusive to the legitimate consumers. For years, they have been playing that game of keeping the piracy below a certain level while ensuring that the protection measures are not that expensive in a generalized sense, and that includes intrusion on legitimate rights.

The Hack Watch News, which I used to monitor quite a bit, covered what happened when the purveyors of one of these protection systems tried using a renewal technique. As described in an exercise recently with DirecTV, some people had businesses selling hacker versions of smart cards, which were better designed than some of the legitimate smart cards. They gave you access to material that you should not have been allowed to access.[1] Then the algorithms were changed, and the hackers defeated the countermeasure. The algorithms were changed again the second month.[2] After the third time, the Hack Watch News said there was a pall of defeat. The hackers basically gave up.

---

[1] Milo Medin said there was a market for these cards in Canada, because residents there could not subscribe to the programming legally.

[2] Bob Schloss noted that this approach works for new content only. New content requires the new algorithm, which may never be broken or may take a few months to be broken.

I taught a course on some of these things, and I had a cartoon in which a little kid is crying, "Mommy, mommy, I can't get the Cartoon Channel any more." The mother says, "Well, we'll just have to wait until next month when the solution to the next countermeasure is available." The idea is to keep the legitimate service level, for most people, better than that available from the pirate. There are things that we can learn from that approach, although this problem was different from the one at hand here.[3] The satellite pirates were commandeering part of the legitimate system, either for their own benefit as individuals or, in some cases, as part of a business selling smart cards.

We use a secured virtual machine that is independent of the browser.[4] We keep changing it to defeat the hackers. This method is problematic because we have to get that thing on the desktop. We are arranging to get that capability in all of the forward-looking systems, but we do not have a deal with Microsoft so it is problematic within Internet Explorer. There is reasonably good technology such that, as long as you are connected intermittently, it will allow you to do that. Marimba's Castanet software does a good job; you tune in to an upgrade channel. I think Real Network uses either Castanet or something similar. It tells you if an upgrade is available, and then gives you an option, which is the standard way of dealing with this. To make our system effective, you would not allow the option for the upgrade. The problem is raising the stakes on who gets the update, so renewability and tamper resistance are essential.

Napster is having a problem now with legacy content. They are trying to put together a system that will use name tagging to prevent distribution of copyrighted material through Napster. Of course, there are already dozens of ways to counteract that approach. But there is also the concept of requiring proof of origination. There are sophisticated systems that check for proof using cryptography techniques. (Hackers do not target these techniques, but rather try to turn off the structure of the secure system, the key management and things like that.) In the case of something like proof of origination, you must have a policy that says, "This system will not read or present any data that lacks proof of origination." In which case you would have secure labels and so on. You will still have

---

Thus, even with a great system, all the old pornography produced before a certain date—a lot of material—still would be available for everyone to see.

[3]David Forsyth said the problem is different because the satellite pirates are "vicarious" content providers who are not doing anything to their own satellites. They might hack your chips, whereas anyone who gains access to pornography on the Internet can distribute it.

[4]David Forsyth suggested that software vendors might give out new browsers every couple of months to defeat the hackers. But it is not clear that everyone is jumping on the rendered software bandwagon.

the issue of what to do about unlabeled content, whether legacy material or not. You need a policy that deals with unlabeled content.

People believe they should get satellite programming or music from Napster for free[5] because the data are not stored in any encrypted way when someone buys it. This is a fundamental issue. For new things, you can use the lack of an "in the clear" distribution path as the exclusion mechanism; this is the issue with the record industry. But from the perspective of media, do you believe that this type of structure, which, in essence, rents content or distributes rights according to content, will be any more successful outside of the commerce space, where you can basically say, "If you want to do this, then you have to do it this way"? Do you believe that this will ever be successful given all the history?

I am making an actual personal bet that it will. But the path to getting there will not be easy. I look at the forces that resist success and wonder whether they can be overcome. I have spent a lot of time thinking about privacy because of the issue of collecting information about events in distributed systems. I do not think we will have a truly productive distributed computing system unless we know how we can collect information about those events. We are dealing with that in the embedded systems committee. At my company, we say, "Collected information about those things is protected, and we have techniques and policy mechanisms to do that." How effective we can make them and how can we use distributed trust mechanisms? We know that we cannot do it perfectly, but this does not mean we do not try.

There is also interplay between law enforcement and policy at the government level. In the DRM field, we depend on things such as the Digital Millennium Copyright Act, with which I was not completely happy because of its impact on research. But certain aspects of it are reasonable. Its provisions are important—addressing issues associated with countermeasures, and what risks you take when you try to defeat a countermeasure. If we could get the research aspect right, then I would be happy. There are also other things, such as copyright and patent law.

If you are a purveyor of mechanisms that defeat countermeasures, what consequences do you face? What are the risks? My house does not

---

[5]Winnie Wechsler said that in the mid-1980s, when encryption was introduced to the backyard satellite dish market for the first time (before DirecTV), there was an uproar among people who owned e-band satellite dishes, because they felt it was their right to have access to this programming, which had always been free. They bought the dish, and the free programming was part of the proposition. Then suddenly programmers started to use encryption, and there was a huge backlash involving piracy. She suggested that this is a fundamental hurdle in developing any solution to piracy.

have a lot of security systems. Many other people have all types of security systems on their houses. Yet it is very simple to deal with them; you could level a house with a bulldozer, for example, and grab the jewelry. This does not happen because we have laws and law enforcement. The same type of situation will occur here. The cost of the systems clearly has to fall,[6] and you need a shared infrastructure so that, instead of just a few people paying for it, a lot of people pay a much smaller per-person price for it. This is why the techniques will not be rolled out just yet.

There are solutions coming in a couple of years that will use more sophisticated distributed trust management techniques to increase the barriers to unauthorized redistribution of content.[7] This will be done on the basis of actions that firms can insist that you do as a condition of receiving their material. I believe this to be true because many larger publishers—including entertainment publishers, such as Time Warner, Universal, Bertelsmann, and Reuters—are funding the establishment of some of these mechanisms.

---

[6]Robin Raskin said the cost of the system would exceed the costs of the music or television show that one tried to protect. He gave the example of publishers dealing with authors' contracts. In looking at DRM, he decided it was cheaper in the short term (the next 2 years) to pay all the authors more money than to implement a rights management system, the costs of which, for a big publishing company, would be astronomical. Herb Lin said representatives of the adult online industry told the committee that they have problems with people copying their content and redistributing it without paying. He said it seemed doubtful that any single provider could afford to implement a DRM system. Bob Schloss said DRM would work in the music industry because the major labels believe that each artist is unique, such that almost nothing is a substitute. This may not be the case for other types of content, including pornography. If Danni Ashe (who testified before the committee at a previous meeting) required a special browser plug-in or keyword every time someone visited her site, and no one else had such a requirement and her competitors were comparable, then people would go elsewhere. John Rabun said most of Ashe's images are copied all over the place. The people who copy them do not even bother to change the titles, even though you would expect that someone violating a copyright would at least do this. Rabin said Ashe expressed concern about new talent, but this constitutes probably less than 1 percent of all adult pornography sites.

[7]John Blumenthal said he checked the Web site of Danni Ashe to see how she did age verification and how she contained her content to her site. Then he went to Usenet, where some news groups focus on her. The news groups—at least three or four different Usenet servers—contained no images of her. Somehow she is creating a barrier between her Web site and Usenet. Herb Lin said he asked Ashe these questions and she is very concerned about redistribution; she also hired her own technical staff to deal with the issue. David Forsyth said he does not understand why she does this, because it is valuable when people redistribute low-resolution or inconvenient versions of good content. Forsyth is finishing a textbook, which can be downloaded in PDF format and printed. It is much less convenient to print an 800-page book than to buy it, but availability of the PDF version means that everyone gets to look at it.

12.3 SUMMARY

Carrying out the concepts of trust and policy management is not trivial. We need languages and ways in which we can identify principals. In some of this space, we need to identify principals in an anonymous way. P3P addresses some of this, but I am not sure whether it will do everything that we want without things like exception mechanisms. We need credentials and an artificial intelligence compliance checker. These are not universally available, but there is a drive to make them more available because of their usefulness in commerce. Until these things are embedded in such a way that people interact with automated systems in a natural fashion, it is difficult to believe that the mechanisms will have widespread effectiveness. Some of the research needs to focus on how people interact with these systems.

InterTrust has embedded a trust management system that adheres to these principles into the systems deployed on behalf of its partners. We also play another important role. There must be an administrator; someone has to be copyrighted as the root source of trust. This must be a utility-like function, that is, carried out by someone who specializes in doing these types of things and does not compete with the people for whom these mechanisms are deployed, because there could be bias.

Do we have competitors? Yes, we have competitors. In spaces such as music, our main competitor is Microsoft, which, interestingly enough, does not have the utility-like attribute. Microsoft competes with many service providers, which is what they (the service providers) are afraid of (in making Microsoft a gatekeeper, through their DRM). People expect InterTrust, as an impartial trusted party, not to compete with them as we deploy these types of mechanisms. We are putting legal structures in place to ensure that this happens. DRM is all that we do. We charge a utility fee, which I think is 60 basis points on transactions that use the technology. The reason the Universal music group, Bertelsmann, and a few others have looked kindly on us is because of our impartiality in that we do not compete with them. But we have also heard that they think that 60 basis points is a "cheap date."

13

Problems with a Dot-xxx Domain

Donald Eastlake

I co-wrote a personal Internet draft in the Internet Engineering Task Force (IETF) about the problems with mandatory labeling.[1] People often come up with ideas about how to segregate or label all bad material to magically solve the content selection or child protection problem. This idea is simple and easy to understand, but it does not work. There are a lot of problems with it, which this draft tries to summarize. The problems can be divided into several categories.

The first category of problems is philosophical. The idea of finding a way to categorize content in the global context of the Internet is absurd. There are 200 countries and they all have different laws. For example, laws on nude modeling differ. In one country you can have a magazine consisting entirely of nude pictures of 17-year-olds, but this is obviously a felonious and criminal act in another country, where nude models have to be 18. Yet another country might not permit any noticeable amount of the female body under any circumstances in a magazine or publication. There is no hope of getting a consistent point of view on this sort of thing. And this is just one criterion.

Moreover, there are more cultures than there are countries. There are literally thousands of cultures, all of which have their own particular

---

[1]See <ftp://ftp.ietf.org/internet-draft/draft-eastlake-xxx-00.txt>. Personal Internet drafts have no formal status and are not endorsed by the IETF or any other group. The draft is intended to become an informational request for comments (RFC), a document that is issued under the auspices of the IETF.

quirks and ideas regarding what sorts of things children should be allowed to access or the age at which children become adults. Going one step further, the concept of community has made it easier to develop standards, one way or another. But there are literally millions of communities.

Another category of problems is legal. If you require everyone who has a certain type of content to be in the dot-xxx name space, then you are, in effect, forcing speech on them. This seems to be a problem with respect to certain legal rights in the United States and some other countries. It obviously depends on the circumstances and whether this sort of speech is commercial or noncommercial, and so on. But, in effect, you are requiring people to label themselves, which runs into legal problems and effectively limits their free speech.

One difficulty in thinking about this sort of thing is the malleable nature of the Internet. Some parts of it are similar to commercial broadcast television, which, at least in the United States, currently has a system of labeling. But other parts of the Internet are more like someone strolling through a park and talking to whomever they bump into—activities that are entirely noncommercial, spontaneous, and unorganized. Imagine, if you are strolling through a property and bump into someone and you want to say something that some people could construe as objectionable, that you had to wear a large, yellow star. I think people would consider this to be objectionable. In some respects, labeling of Internet content could be considered similar to the yellow star.

Another category of problems is technical. The labeling system has to be realistic. The use of dot-xxx is not linguistically complicated. But if you try to label in an understandable way the various different axes of heresy or derogatory speech—whatever people object to—then you would have problems with the language from which to select the labeling. In addition, the Internet is not technically structured for things to be done in this way. The Internet has a hierarchically distributed control structure, so that one entity controls dot-com, for example, and other entities control the subzones below dot-com. There are multiple levels. Typically what is identified by one of these names is an IP address for some machine that can store data. Of course, we worry about causing a name to somehow correspond to some characteristic of the data in that machine. In fact, the people controlling these different name zones are likely to be independent organizations, and there is no way to stop other people from pointing at your material.

In other words, if you post material on a Web site with a name, there is no technical mechanism to stop someone else who has independent control of a different zone on the Internet from posting a pointer to your IP address under any name that they choose. If you have innocent material, there is no way to stop someone from creating a dot-xxx name that points to your project. Similarly, if you have material that is placed correctly in dot-xxx, there is no way to stop someone from creating an innocent-sounding name that points to you. If we had global laws, we could make this practice illegal and go round up all of the people who do it and fine them.

All of these tricks are affordable. It is very simple, for example, to take an arbitrary mailing list, one that is entirely innocent and devoted to some light topic, and create an alternative address that you can send mail to, an address with terrible things about "xxx" in its name. You can have this bad sounding address automatically forward messages to the real, innocent mailing list and change the envelope information—things not normally seen around a message—and the headers. There is no software that checks on these functions, so it is easy to cause things to be distributed to individuals or mailing lists while making it appear that the mailing list has a name that is actually forged. In principle, a few of these problems could be solved by globally distributing changed software, but this is unlikely to happen.

There are other things on the Internet that have domain names that are not really domain names. For example, there is Net News, which has news groups that are hierarchically named but not hierarchically structured. They are more anarchic than domain names because they do not have a root and so on. They are more like a conversation, in that anyone could post anything to any of these news groups and, except for the few that are moderated, it is not clear how you can enforce much control over the names. Similarly, names are used in Internet relay chat and chat rooms that are also very conversation-like. Given all of this, you wonder if you can reasonably come up with an approach that would meet reasonable linguistic criteria and somehow affect all of these different naming schemes in any reasonable fashion.

There is nothing wrong with the mere existence of a dot-xxx domain name,[2] or with just anybody getting a dot-xxx site. But I feel that, if such a category existed, it would greatly increase the probability of laws requiring people to register there. This is not a technical problem, and there

---

[2]Milo Medin said that some companies want to brand themselves in such a way, and this mechanism is convenient. Logically, if there were a generic law that said people had to label themselves, it would be universally agreed that, if people put their content into dot-xxx, they should not be prosecuted if a child happened to get in there and the filtering software failed. Dot-xxx is not the way to enforce mandatory labeling; this should be done with PICS or something page dependent. However, someone could be prosecuted, either civilly or criminally, if they put not-for-minors content into a dot-kids domain.

is certainly no technical difficulty with the mere existence of that utility and the ability of people to get names there, as long as some organization runs a registry for it. There is a slippery slope argument, but it is not currently mentioned in our draft. The main thrust of our draft is to provide a convenient, precompiled answer for people who assert that a mandatory dot-xxx domain name will magically solve the problem they perceive in the categorization of Internet content.

The idea of a dot-kids domain may have a different spin in various ways. It still has the problem that the criteria for what kids are and what is appropriate material for them differ widely among nations, cultures, and communities. But in some sense it is a little better than dot-xxx. Maybe if you put something in dot-kids that is not considered appropriate for children, you would be prosecuted.

I also want to comment on the idea, which is mentioned less often, of categorizing content with a bit of the IP address. All hosts on the Internet have either 32-bit addresses under IPV-4 or 128-bit addresses under IPV-6, which is not widespread but is getting some attention. There are many problems with this approach. It is, in some ways, coarser than the domain names (sometimes the main name structures can be used to address a subset of material for the host). In some sense, like the address of a building, it refers to everything in that building. One problem is that there are no extra bits in IPV-4. Taking even one bit away would cause havoc; there are not enough addresses to go around. The whole reason for the creation of IPV-6 was to overcome the limit of 32 bits in IPV-4.

Another problem is that these bits are not arbitrary. They are topologically significant. As packets are sent through the network, they are routed by comparing the prefix bits on these numbers with a routing table. Essentially, the longest match determines how the packet is sent. I am simplifying this a bit, but at the top level of the Internet, routing tables currently have on the order of 40,000 or 50,000 entries, and this determines where things go at the top level, and they trickle down from there until they get to a particular local machine. If you assign addresses randomly, then you need billions of routes at the top level or else it would not work. There is no feasible hardware today that understands how to do this. For the Internet to work and get the data around, the address bits have to be assigned in a topologically meaningful way, directly related to the actual structure of the Internet and how the IPs are connected to each other.

IPV-6 might sound more hopeful, but it is not. One popular proposal, intended to enable wide deployment, effectively would reduce the routing part of the IPV-6 address to half of the full size. In this scheme, 64 bits would be used for all of the routing control, and the other 64 bits would be used as a unique end-point identifier. Conceivably, you could somehow get one bit out of the bottom of the 64. But once you consider the need to label things along all the different dimensions and categories you might need on a globally meaningful basis, there is no way to do it in the bits in an IP address.

There is some hope for a technical solution. PICS has multiple modes. The mode in which you have to put a fixed label on your Web page or site has all types of similar problems as does forced speech, and not enough categories, and so on. But PICS does have a mode in which you have separate servers, like a separate rating service. You can ask the servers about certain data, certain sites, and so forth. This, at least, seems not to have the problems of forced speech or the limitations of other labels. You could have literally thousands or millions of different PICS servers that painted the world in different ways, and they would enable you to ask questions as to whether certain parts of the network are approved or not by the vendor of that particular PICS rating service, which could be some particular church, culture, or country. I am not saying that this necessarily would work wonderfully, but it does seem to have at least some technical practicality.

14

Business Dimensions: The Education Market

Irv Shapiro

I am the chief executive officer for Edventions, which provides a suite of software services and training to introduce technology transparently into schools. Let me define "transparent" very simply. When you got into your car this morning, all you needed to do was hold onto the steering wheel, push two pedals (maybe three, if you are an advanced driver), and you were done. You did not think about what type of engine was in the car, why it worked, or any of those kinds of issues—the car was transparent technology.[1]

14.1 THE ROLE OF TEACHERS

I am most interested in the role of teachers in elementary schools, which are very different from high schools or universities. From a business perspective, teachers are both an asset and a liability. That asset and liability may be the solution to some of the questions posed earlier today (described earlier in these proceedings).

For at least 2,600 years, from the time of the Greek academies, when adults have wanted to introduce children to new material, they have sent

---

[1]Sandra Calvert noted that driving a car is not transparent for a new driver. When first learning to drive, she was concerned about what to do if she had to sneeze. This is something that requires thought; it is not an automatic skill. Even today, she carries an American Automobile Association card so that she can call emergency services if she runs into any problems.

them to school. Teachers are expected to teach more than reading, writing, and arithmetic. We also expect teachers to make decisions. Teachers have immense classroom autonomy. In elementary schools, the number of supervisory staff is small compared to the number of teaching staff, and teachers in the classroom are mostly on their own. They decide—we trust them to decide—what our children should learn each day. In that process, they make many selections.

The same processes are at work in the elementary school library. The library does not have a million books in it. Even if the school could afford a million books, having a million books would not be a good idea. For example, if a third grader is writing a book report on George Washington and goes to the library and finds a thousand books on the shelf about him, the student will sit on the ground and begin to cry. I have four children; I know this to be a fact. School librarians and teachers select books for the library under the direction of the school board, state and federal standards, and recommendations from organizations.

14.2 HISTORICAL PERSPECTIVE

The challenge is how to provide the tools that teachers need to lead and teach children in the Internet age. The present rate of technology change is unprecedented in history. The impact of information technology is comparable to the impact of Gutenberg's printing press at the end of the 1400s, but today the impact is being manifested over several years instead of several decades.

How do we empower teachers? Let us look at the last 30 years. Over the last 10 years, there has been universal agreement that the economy has been robust. Even with the adjustments occurring now (I am no expert, and I do not know if they are permanent or if this is a recession), times have been good for 10 years.

When economists looked at this period of time, they were baffled initially, because, as I learned years ago in Economics 101, you cannot have both low inflation and low unemployment. You cannot have robust growth, low interest rates, and a full employment economy. Those things do not happen together; they have to be kept in balance. The Federal Reserve Board kept them all in balance, and taxes kept them in balance. Economists eventually concluded that there was a dramatic increase in productivity over that period of time as a result of the introduction of computer technology into the American economy. That increase in productivity allowed us to produce more goods for less cost.

This sounds wonderful. But I was in steel mills in the mid-1970s installing computers, and I guarantee you that there was no increase in productivity. When we walked into the mills, they laughed about all the people they were going to have to hire to take care of the computers doing their payroll, general ledger, and accounts receivable. Maybe the computers were controlling a couple of machines, monitoring temperatures of furnaces, and doing process control, but there was no increase in productivity.

Let us assume, for the sake of argument, that there was no increase in productivity in the 1970s. Yet in the 1990s, the economy was robust. What changed? Some very smart people and organizations, such as SAP, Microsoft Corporation, Apple Computer, and Sun Microsystems, recognized that the computers in the plants, factories, and offices of America would not account for the difference. Nor would it come from the infrastructure. No, the difference was that these companies began to build specialized software for industry, and businesses invested hundreds of millions of dollars in training their workforces. In the 1970s, we put in lots of wires and computers; in the 1980s, we introduced new software designed to revolutionize the process of manufacturing. The word processor changes peoples' lives.

I have two children in college who would not even know how to write a paper in longhand. This is a technologically revolutionary time. So where does technology stand in the schools? Because of the E-Rate and other successful programs, we have put lots of computers and wires into the schools. But it seems to me that the schools are stuck in the 1970s because we have not retrained our teachers. We have not introduced new software specifically designed for these markets—especially for elementary school. Instead, we have taken software designed for the business community, universities, or high schools, and tried to roll it downhill to a second-grade classroom.

Teachers in second grade do not have $5,000 projectors. They may have laptop computers, but PowerPoint and Excel are not tools for them. The teachers need something different. Thus, the opportunity for the business community now is the same opportunity that existed at the end of the 1970s for the traditional computer and software companies. There is a need for software and training in the schools. There is a need for help desks so that teachers can pick up a telephone and talk to a real person at 8:00 P.M. or 11:00 P.M. without being put on hold for an hour, as they try to prepare an assignment for the next day. This is a wonderful business opportunity, which is why I got involved with it $2\,^1/_2$ years ago.

14.3　THE SCHOOL MARKETPLACE

The other side of the story is that teachers are scared. They are underpaid and overworked. When a teacher gives our children more homework, the teacher has more homework the next night, too. They get calls late at night. They work in a complex environment. Quite candidly, the skills that make someone a phenomenal second-grade teacher are probably not skills that would enable them to deal with such complexity. Change in the elementary school education marketplace is difficult, because teachers do not want anything to do with it. Our company has been involved in many districts where the superintendents and principals brought in a program but the teachers dug in their heels and said, "No, we will not use this stuff. We do not even want to learn it."[2]

It will take some time. Unfortunately, the cost of time is dollars. In this economy that has just survived the dot-com world, think about time in terms of months, maybe a year and a fraction. When you talk to the investment community about going into a marketplace in which you may have to spend 2 years in a sales and educational process, providing education at a subsidized rate, the investment community says, "There are easier places to put our money."

Why should they do it? Because switching costs—to use economic terms—in the schools are very high. Once a program is in a school, it does not go away. If I had a magic wand, I would look at how to pump dollars into teacher education and the creation of software and technology specifically targeted to this marketplace, even though we know the payback probably will take 5 years instead of 18 months. The reason to do it is that the marketplace is very large. Look at the President's budget and see the large numbers going into education. When you are in the market and are successful, you provide very good returns to investors.

Whether you do that as a nonprofit, whether the government does it, or whether the government provides funds to a for-profit to do it, it is a fundamental issue. As a for-profit attempting to address that need, we find it very difficult to raise capital, because the return on investment takes longer than the current capital markets want. This is not just a private market problem. Look at the allocation of federal funds. As an example, E-Rate was strictly a program for lines and hardware. The way you get Title 1 dollars to apply to technology is to repackage the technology as reading, math, and basic learning. The overall challenge is to find a way to retrain the teachers—not put dollars into curriculum, hardware,

---

[2]Sandra Calvert said teachers today are expected to do much more than teach. They are expected to solve social problems, such as parents getting divorced. Then the computer is thrown in. A teacher using a computer to give a presentation needs to become a technical expert in case something goes wrong. If it breaks down, then usually a whole classroom of kids is left sitting there, because technical support is seldom available in the classroom.

and lines, which is where I see the majority of the dollars going. Some federal money is targeted specifically to professional development, but look at the order of magnitude difference between professional development and hardware and infrastructure.

Over the past 2 years, many businesses looked at the size of the pot in the education marketplace and attempted to fill the gap by using advertising revenues or other nontraditional revenue sources. They failed. We are left with two models, which may be fine. Very large corporations have a vested interest in the current model. They would like teachers to use textbooks in the exact same way as in the past; they are not interested in the technology changing too rapidly. These parties have deep pockets, which is okay. There is also the continual opportunity marathon, in which someone can start a small business and leave it as a small business. In a number of sectors of elementary schools' infrastructure, there are many small "mom and pop" operations that never grow beyond serving the technology needs of a couple of communities.

Teachers' unions have no effect, positive or negative. In the long term, they could have a slight positive influence. But in the situations that we have seen over the past 30 months, this has rarely been packaged as a union issue. Every once in a while we hear, "Our contract is coming up in 6 months and we do not want any change until the contract is renegotiated." There are many fearful teachers out there, and getting them over that fear is as massive an undertaking as the complete E-Rate undertaking. This is much more expensive than what we have done on the technology side. Unions could be a positive force in helping their membership to overcome this fear.[3]

There is another positive force coming. The statistics indicate that about 50 percent of the teachers in America are approaching retirement age, and as many as 50 percent will retire over the next 5 years. The people going into those jobs probably recently came from universities where they got all of their homework online and computers were used transparently, so they may demand this in the schools. Teachers become

---

[3]Janet Schofield suggested that unions could be helpful in negotiating, for example, discounts for teachers buying home computers. In studying teachers, she has found that, if they have computers at home, they are more likely to get over their initial reluctance. Maybe sons or daughters train them, and they have more time in the home environment. Unions could reduce the economic barriers and create centers for their members to get home computers. She also suggested that teacher training relates directly to other issues at hand. For example, teachers seldom know enough about the Internet to realize how they might prepare kids to surf safely and responsibly. Teachers may not know how to locate good sites that will draw the kids in.

obsolete because we have not done our job of training them. If we had done our job better as a society of providing teachers with the expertise and training that they needed, then society would not have to solve this other issue of kids' access to inappropriate material. Teachers are very influential, at least with very young children.

We need to develop a business model that takes a patient approach to the retraining of the teacher workforce.[4] Over the last 9 months, we have held training in 200 schools in Internet access, how to select good sites, how to use our particular tools, and a variety of related topics. We no longer will be doing on-site, in-service training. Instead, we are moving to a model in which we will train a trainer in the school and provide a variety of multimedia materials for the teachers. We have found that what is most effective with teachers is "just in time" training, rather than bringing them into an in-service for a day at the beginning of the year and then 4 months later when they go to use the materials. Providing that type of training and support mechanisms is expensive. It is a challenge to develop business models that will support the teachers so that they can provide the education that will cut down on some of the bad things that happen in this networked world.

---

[4]Marilyn Mason said that when libraries began using the Internet, entire staffs were retrained. Librarians are neither more nor less reluctant to use technology than are teachers. But if a library had something very specific that it wanted the staff to do, and if librarians saw this as a way to make their jobs easier and make themselves more effective, then they could embrace the technology as a new tool. The education profession has not sorted out how the Internet can be a tool for improving education. Mason suggested looking at where one can intervene in a cycle. One opportunity may be the emphasis on test scores, because they provide some measure of effectiveness. There are software packages that help children learn to read, and they can be effective if used in libraries. The key is to make sure there is a common understanding of how teachers are supposed to use technology.

15

Business Models: Kid-Friendly Internet Businesses

Brian Pass

Until yesterday, I was president, chief executive officer, and cofounder of Passport New Media, which created a product called "Your Own World" (YOW for short), stand-alone software designed to enable children to experience third-party Internet content in a protected, offline environment. For parents, we offered peace of mind that their kids, when using our software, would never be exposed to the dangers of the Internet. For kids, we dramatically improved the performance of the Internet by eliminating bandwidth constraints and putting all of the content on the personal computer (PC).

We founded the company in January 1999. We were a year in development, building this software from scratch. We launched the product last spring but, when we went to raise our third round of capital and market the product nationwide, we were hit by the financing problems that face many companies these days. Bankruptcy papers were filed just yesterday. Nonetheless, we are proud of the product, which drew a lot of praise from parents, especially, and from critics who covered the space.

I am also a father of two girls aged 5 and 7, and many of my comments are informed by the fact that I am a concerned parent.

15.1 BUILDING AN INTERNET BUSINESS

What are the primary challenges of building a business based on the idea of attracting kids to safe and appropriate Internet content? Building any Internet-based business is difficult, but especially in the kids' space. The kids' companies suffer from all the same problems that the adult-content companies do, but the problems are exacerbated. The problems are not necessarily different in nature, except for the safety area.

The first and biggest challenge is the Internet itself, which is not necessarily an effective medium for young children aged 2 to 12, especially for those under 10. The bandwidth constraints pose one of the most significant problems. Even at broadband speeds, children find content coming over the Internet frustrating. Adults do, too. If you try to watch a video or animation, especially over a dial-up connection but even over broadband connections, the experience is not pleasant. It is tolerable for adults but becomes intolerable for kids. This is a business challenge because of the competition. You are competing with TV, video games that perform extremely well, and PC software that works well. When you click on a PC game, something happens right away; the same cannot be said for content coming over the Internet.

A snowballing series of other business challenges arise out of these bandwidth constraints. There are creative limitations on what you can do in a space. If you want to do something that works well over the Internet, chances are you will make creative sacrifices that make your content fare worse than your competition. This applies to entertainment-based content and educational content. Our product was somewhere in the middle, in the edu-tainment space. The creative trade-offs pose real challenges.

Many companies have tried to develop original educational content and deliver it exclusively over the Internet. For example, MaMaMedia in New York tried to create bandwidth-intensive educational (but fun) content for kids. They were challenged from a business perspective because they spent a lot of money marketing this product. There was a major mass-advertising campaign of which my kids were well aware; they asked me if we could buy Fruit Roll-ups so that they could get the secret code for a game on a MaMaMedia site—notwithstanding the fact that they are not allowed on the Internet and have never seen MaMaMedia. This was a successful campaign and it drove millions of unique visitors to the site. But from a business perspective, those kids did not visit the site often or stay very long, and the performance results were probably among the worst in the industry of the companies that I am aware.

At Passport, we tried to address this very issue by bringing the content off the Internet and making it perform well. As a consequence, we did not have the same problems. On average, our kids visited 10 times a month and stayed 25 minutes each time they sat down, about 10 times the industry rate (kids visiting less than twice a month and staying maybe 25 minutes during the entire month). We had other problems, but bandwidth clearly is holding kids back from embracing the Internet in important ways.

The other major limitations of the Internet include the safety and privacy concerns. I will address them from a business perspective. The first issue is the cost of complying with regulations. The Children's On-Line Privacy Protection Act governs this space. There have been many discussions since the law was enacted about the costs, in dollars, that these regulations impose on content providers. These are just some of the costs of doing business in this space.

The more important cost is the primal fear factor. I do not wish to question parents' judgment, because I share a lot of those concerns. But parents' fear of the Internet makes it a less than great medium for the simple reason they do not allow their younger kids online in great numbers. (I am not referring to teenagers, who embrace the Internet in much higher numbers.) When you combine this fact with the unpleasant, bandwidth-constrained online experience for kids—if they are allowed online—it explains why fewer than one in three kids who have Internet access at home are actually online. (This number does not include kids who access the Internet from schools.)

Another major challenge to a business seeking to provide content to kids in a safe way is financing. This is obviously the biggest issue facing Internet companies of any type today, but even when we got started in early 1999, during the glory days of the Internet, the kids' segment was difficult for the venture capital community. I cannot tell you how many times I was in a venture capital meeting and was told, "It is very difficult to monetize kids." As repugnant as that sounds, it gets to the heart of the problem. There is no bigger challenge than getting a business funded and off the ground. Even in the late 1990s, the industries serving children were not doing especially well. This includes television production, historically a difficult business, and the CD-ROM business, which is very hit driven and a difficult retail model. The Learning Company, then under Mattel, was struggling in those days, and I read just recently that, since the company was sold, it has reached the break-even point.

15.2 COMPARING BUSINESS MODELS

After the stock market crash of last year, I did not hear about the issue of monetizing children anymore in meetings, because I was not getting any meetings. I could not have presented a worse business model to the venture capital community last year—I think the same still holds for today—because the model embraces content for kids and has an advertising-supported revenue stream.

One might argue that the business case has not yet been made for providing content to kids in a safe way. But many people have tried. The business models today can be categorized by two variables. The first variable is the market that you are targeting, such as kids in the home, the consumer market, or kids in schools. These are different markets and are dividing lines among business models. The second variable is the revenue model, whether ad-supported or fee-based subscription or licensing. I am excluding e-commerce.

If you constructed a matrix using those variables, you would have consumer ad-supported companies, consumer subscription-fee companies, school-based ad-supported companies, and school-based subscription-fee companies. We were in the first of those four categories, with a consumer product for the home supported by advertising. Other examples of this type are MaMaMedia, Zeeks, FreeZone, and probably a host of others.

The problems here with the business case are similar to those facing sites for adults: the high cost of creating content, slow acceptance by advertisers, and limitations of the Internet medium with respect to advertising. Not only does it make for a poor entertainment content experience, but it also makes for a poor advertising experience. The traditional form of advertising on the Web is a banner ad, which you click and it takes you to another site. For a kid, especially over a dial-up modem, that form of advertising is a nonstarter. The kid gets lost when transferred to another site. Even the content provider loses out, because now the kid is no longer at the original site. It is a losing proposition all the way around.

We tried to address this problem with offline capability. Instead of kids clicking on a banner ad and going to another site, they got a rich media pay-off right away. They could play a game instantly. They could watch the full, $2\,^1/_2$-minute Rocky and Bullwinkle movie trailer behind a banner ad that played in real time with no bandwidth constraints. Not surprisingly, we got a very high response to that ad. But with a small user base, you cannot make a lot of money doing this. This was our big challenge; we could not build a base big enough to get large advertisers on board, even though they were excited about the product. We did not have enough kids for them to reach. We did not build the base quickly enough before we ran out of cash. Timing is everything, and that had a lot to do with it.

There are many examples of the consumer-subscription model in the kids' space, such as JuniorNet, probably the closest technically to what we were doing, and Disney Blast. These companies have tried to offer subscription-based services to kids in the home, such that the subscription takes the form of a monthly or yearly fee. The problem is that the subscription model never has worked for any Internet company, as far as I know. Many people have tried to charge for content, but people at home feel that Internet content should be free of charge. This has been the fundamental problem of the Internet for all companies, not just those catering to kids.

An example of a school business model that adopted an advertising approach would be Zap Me, which offered to wire schools and build infrastructure in exchange for being able to advertise or market to children in those schools. This brings up difficult issues in terms of the commercialization of schools. Zap Me found that it was unworkable and the company no longer deals with schools or kids; it is now offering network services under a different name, rStar Networks.

The fourth model in the matrix is school-based services that use a subscription or licensing model. This is the predominant model. Classroom Connect, Light Span, and others have developed online, fee-based services for schools. We have heard a lot about the obstacles and difficulties of working in schools; I will highlight just a few.

One difficulty is the great variability in how networks and computers are structured. Every school is a little bit different in ways that affect how you bring content into that school. Statistics show a very high penetration of Internet access in schools, but I doubt that any one school is like any other in the way that kids use and experience the Internet. Some have computers in the classrooms, others have them only in the library, and still others have a separate computer lab. This makes it very difficult to create curriculum-based content.

In addition, there is an underlying assumption that learning from the PC or the Internet is a good thing, especially in schools. This remains to be shown. I believe that, on the whole, my kids are better off. They are learning to use software and have had positive experiences on computers. But at least some studies suggest that this is not necessarily a good thing, so this becomes a barrier to successfully putting content into those schools.

Ultimately, the successful model (if there is one) will do the following things: It will work well within the bandwidth limitations of the Internet. It will focus on what the Internet does well, which is deliver content and exchange text. It will meet the demands of parents. It will be safe, secure, and private. And, above all, it will meet the demands of kids, the toughest ones to please in this market. It will entertain, it will educate, and it will be well done so that they will accept it.

No one has tried yet to shrink-wrap a content-based Web product—the publisher's model. CD-ROM developers are trying to incorporate the Internet into their off-the-shelf products. We could have shrink-wrapped our product and put it on a shelf. But at the time, we looked at the companies doing this and saw the difficulties that they were having. The Learning Company and others in the educational space had difficult distribution models and had to provide incentives for purchases by offering very substantial rebates. The publishing model was not attractive to us at the time. Maybe Netscape tried this model when they first introduced the Navigator.[1]

There are also other issues. One is whether a company in this space can be grown organically while avoiding some of the venture capital funding issues. It probably can. Somewhere, there is probably someone creative enough to make their own educational or entertainment content, post it on the Web, and build a business that can pay for itself over time. I was not smart enough to go about it this way, but I think someone may succeed.

Sadly, some of the best sites for kids on the Web are probably the commercial ones pushing products. Nabisco, LifeSavers, and Kellogg's are examples of dynamic, well-done sites that exist purely to promote products. They have great activities. The most popular game that circulated around our office was a Tetris-like game with Fruit Loops; it was a lot of fun. Unfortunately, this is where the money is. They have a different purpose in bringing that content to kids, and they can afford to create beautiful stuff.

Businesses targeting 12- to 18-year-olds would face a lot of the same challenges. The Web applications are different—more chat, more instant messaging—and the content is different. I have not seen as much educational content going to teens. The content is more like the Back Street Boys, surfing, and skateboarding. The companies operating in this space have had very mixed results. A notable company in San Francisco, Kibu, recently closed before it ever launched. Bandwidth is less of an issue for teens, who are more tolerant than younger kids and understand the medium better. They are looking to the Internet for different things. There are also more homework issues. Teens who go home and do their homework want to do research and access those positive aspects of the Internet. Any technology change has both good and bad aspects.[2]

---

[1]Marilyn Mason suggested that this model is going in the direction of a journal for a different level of reader.

[2]Irv Shapiro said his company targets the ages between very young children and teens, primarily kids aged 6 to 12. He uses a subscription model paid for by the schools. His motivation is simple: He had good fortune in a previous career, planned to donate about 100 computers to schools, walked around to see how they were planning to use them, and was appalled. This led to the creation of Edventions. The goal was to integrate computers into schools just as calculators had been integrated into the math curriculum, based on the idea that children will use calculators to do arithmetic when they become adults. In the early years, elementary school math teachers were against any use of calculators. Now, calculators are integrated into the curriculum. A division of Texas Instruments is devoted to selling calculators to schools. Similarly, children will use computers as teens in high school and as adults, so the societal motivation is to find the proper way to provide a safe, secure environment for these children to learn about computers. Shapiro's solution is to try to leverage the talents of teachers to do this. Sandra Calvert said Dan Geer sent around a

There has been a lot more business activity in the teen space, and a few companies have gone public. Sites like Bolt, Alloy, and Snowball are really going after this market and these advertising dollars, because teens have more disposable income. They can make decisions. Then the questions become whether they are staying away from pornography and whether marketing to them is good or bad.

I spoke about a year ago at a conference at which there was a heated discussion about the commercialization of the Web and kids. Someone asked why there is nothing like a Public Broadcasting System (PBS) for kids on the Internet. The discussion went on for about 5 or 10 minutes, and it was heated. No one pointed out that PBS is the PBS of the Web—it is out there online. Maybe not enough people know about it, but this may be a good model going forward (it is one that I was toying with late in the game). We could create nonprofit organizations that license commercial technology and work in that space, and corporations that want to do good work can sponsor good educational content. We can have something like PBS; it is not out of the realm of possibility.

In the course of licensing content from major media companies and in dealing with their kids' divisions in separate Internet operating groups, I did not think those separate Internet groups did very well.[3] My sense is that Nickelodeon, for example, went through two or three massive restructurings of its Internet group over the last 2 years. Another example is Warner Brothers, whose online site just folded itself back into the company. Fox is withdrawing from having separate Internet divisions, including Fox for Kids, and wrapping them back up in the network. Television is a great driver. But it is interesting that sites like Nickelodeon or Fox for Kids do no better than the industry averages in terms of repeat visitation and total minutes of use. The media company is making money from the TV show and not necessarily from the Web. They are not that different from Life Savers, which is promoting products online and doing it well.

---

memo about the use of calculators, especially among minority children, who do not understand the fundamentals of math but can use a calculator. This approach needs to be tempered with more basic knowledge. Calculators alone are not a magic bullet for doing math.

[3]Winnie Wechsler suggested that Web sites linked to television networks or other pre-existing media seem to do well. Whatever her kids watch on television, they also use on the Internet. In other words, the business model that works involves a Web site that augments viewership on television, which, in turn, draws traffic to the Web. To address the problem of drawing traffic, what is more powerful than a 24-hour ad on television?

15.3 THE ROLE OF PARENTS

The question of how to deal with inappropriate material goes back to the role of responsible parents. This burden falls on parents, teachers, and librarians by default because the technologies are not strong enough, and the regulatory responses generally run into First Amendment issues about free speech and have a tough time in the courts. By default, responsible adults have to stand up and take the lead in combating inappropriate material.

The central role of responsible adults is the reason why, as businessmen, we made a product that would appeal to parents as the primary decision makers. We demonstrated with the product adoption rates that there is a lot of demand for solutions from parents. Parents are concerned; they want their kids to have a positive Internet experience, and they are searching for solutions.

I do not let my kids go on the Internet without my presence. Of course, they are young (5 and 7), so we will see how vigilant I am in 2 or 3 years. I have a cable modem, and my kids are examples of how bandwidth constraints are a problem. Even when my kids go with me online and we look at something together, they get frustrated and go back to their rooms to play with Barbie dolls. The Internet is slow.

There is concern about whether we want 2- and 3-year-olds on the Internet. By being offline, we could make a completely simplified interface that could be used by 2-year-olds, who did use our service without knowledge of how to use the Internet. I will not say whether this is right or wrong, but the children's educational software industry targets kids starting at that age and even younger. A year or two ago, The Learning Company introduced software that teaches toddlers how to bang on keyboards. My kids were using the computer with multimedia software at 18 months. They are not gifted children. But they happened to be the types of kids who would just as soon be playing outside and would do a little of both. But this is a concern, and it goes back to the assumption that the Internet is a good medium for educating kids. That assumption should be challenged.[4]

---

[4]Sandra Calvert said the issue should be researched. The discussion points to the lack of a database on whether and how little kids should use the Internet. She has seen 4-year-olds who have been online for 2 years, and they are not "hunched over." They are curious; they want to know where the "Back" button is. They are knowledgeable about the Internet. She does not think it is damaging them, but she would pay attention to the sites they visited and whether their parents were with them at the time.

16

Business Models Based on Advertising

Chris Kelly

My presentation will focus on the business models for advertising and commerce on the Internet, still viable despite the general pessimism about the way things are going on the Internet these days. All of the big players have had problems. But there will be a workable business model; the question is how to figure out what it will look like, and how those models can be put to use in protecting kids online.

16.1   COMPARISON OF ADVERTISING MODELS

Advertising will continue to be a significant part of Internet business models, despite what you may hear. There are four basic models for the sale of advertising. The most common models are cost per impression and revenue share, although cost-per-click and cost-per-acquisition deals are gaining in popularity.

Cost-per-impression (CPM) deals are usually experienced as banner ads while you surf the Web. You go to a site such as Excite, and the banner ad is presented to you as part of the page. This is still the bread and butter of the industry, the way most sites generate their major revenues, but it is in serious trouble. Every major Internet portal has seen a serious decline in revenue coming from advertising, and offline businesses dependent on advertising revenues have seen similar thinning.

When banner ads first came out on the Internet, people clicked on them 15 to 20 percent of the time, because nobody knew what they were and everyone was trying to bounce around and figure out this exciting new medium. Things have stabilized now to below half a percent in terms of click rates for a basic banner ad. This has been a disaster in terms of convincing offline advertisers to move some of their budgets online—an effect that everyone has seen on the Nasdaq. In talking about these low clickthrough rates, I am referring to run-of-the-mill ads; I will discuss targeting later.

Because of this lower perceived effectiveness, a few other models are gaining greater prominence, such as "cost per click." Instead of paying for the presentation of your product in a banner advertisement, you pay for the actual clickthrough on the ad. This is less popular and more difficult to negotiate, because Internet networks are reluctant to accept these deals. They say, "If you pay us only on a conversion, on a move, on a redirection to your site, then we cannot forecast what the revenue from this deal is going to be." Advertisers (i.e., ad space owners) are looking for guaranteed payments—generally targeted banner ads.

Cost per lead is a slightly different model. A lead is a conversion so that someone agrees to provide a service or to accept to further direct mail or e-mail—roughly analogous to the response card in a magazine that says, "Circle here for more information."

The revenue share, as I mentioned earlier, is also a popular type of deal. The problem with revenue share deals is that you are depending on actual commerce to pay the bill. If there is no transaction at the end of the day, then revenue does not flow back to the advertising presenter, who is thus not happy about the way the ad space has been used.

16.2 PORTALS, ADVERTISING NETWORKS, AND TARGETING

In discussing advertising-based business models, it's important to note that the big players—America Online, Excite@Home, Yahoo—sell many of their own ads but not all of them, which is important. We have an ad sales force that spends a lot of time going to large advertisers and saying, "For x million dollars, you can get this many impressions on our network. They will be on these particular channels on the network." Smaller players and some of the big ones outsource that type of ad sales to ad networks. The biggest one is Double Click. Other large ones are MatchLogic, a wholly owned subsidiary of our company; Engage; and 24/7 Media. These are third-party networks that operate on a variety of sites across the Internet. Double Click has 2,500 to 3,000 sites from which it serves ads across the Internet. Match Logic has about 1,000 sites. A big concern is the placing of cookies on user's browsers and computers, to track behavior across those different sites.

Targeting is, in many ways, the Holy Grail of the industry. Most ad targeters use profiles based on your behavior across a number of sites within an hour. If you visit 10 or 20 of the 2,500 sites within a Double

Click network, then you get scores associated with each site indicating male or female, likely age, presence of children in the household, and other things like that. Once that profile is established, when you visit a site where ads are served by Double Click, it will read the cookie on your browser and say, "This person is probably between 24 and 35, probably has kids in the household, is probably female, and may have an interest in X." Then you get served an ad that Double Click has sold to an advertiser that matches this demographic profile.

These are usually anonymous, which is an important point. This is one of the biggest sources of confusion and discussion in the privacy arena. The Federal Trade Commission (FTC) took action against Double Click because the company had plans to start personally identifying without user permission. As it turned out, they never did that and the FTC inquiry was properly stopped. They had planned something that probably would have violated the law and it would have been a false incentive advertising practice. But they did not do it.

All of this happens because of the need to drive the click rates up, to actually reach the people that you are trying to target. To the extent that these things are done anonymously, they are, arguably, wonderfully beneficial—and one of the business models that will work. If you can get to the types of people that you want, then it is much easier to present to an advertiser who has x number of dollars to spend to reach this audience, and say, "You should pay this rate, this CPM or whatever, to get these people. Because we know, based on the technology that we've set up, that we can get to people who meet these characteristics."

A number of companies have tried to generate revenues this way. I am sure that a number of the big networks are very involved in ad targeting. This is similar to what grocery stores have been doing by giving out discount cards. The major difference is that the grocery discount cards have personally identifiable data, so that they can send you coupons in the mail.

16.3 CHOICE OF MODELS

Different types of Internet content providers favor different ad models. The quintessential example of the lengths to which some companies will go to drive traffic is that, if you end up accidentally on a porn site, you cannot even close your browser—the site just keeps showing up. Mainstream advertisers are starting to use these technologies, too; if you try to close a window, then ads pop up on a number of different sites. Without having done a full economic study of the porn industry, I cannot say this definitively, but my guess is that they will get hit with some of the same advertising doldrums that everyone else has. The ones making money are probably the ones with subscription models. Porn seems to be one of the few things that people will pay for. The problem in avoiding the content is probably related to promo pages, which are designed to draw people in to pay for a subscription. Filters definitely need to catch those pages.

Most nonporn sites are not trying to show pictures or video, just animations and banner ads, so there is less concern about bandwidth cost in the presentation of screens. One reason why the ad networks have managed to prosper is precisely because their costs are so low.[1] There is a high cost to build servers to push things out and to negotiate the first arrangements with Web sites to build them into the network. But once that happens, you can just serve it out. You added potential customer leads and lowered your customer acquisition cost by expanding your network, because you can send a cookie when a new browser visits a site that has, for example, a Double Click ad. That unique identifier will be carried across every site in the Double Click network and be registered in Double Click. High start-up cost and low marginal cost make a big difference in terms of overall advertising cost.

16.4 ADVERTISING, REGULATION, AND KIDS

There are many questions to be asked about advertising as a model for paying for software or services that would protect kids. The biggest player in filtering in the schools has now abandoned advertising despite the potential for real benefits in terms of a business model and potentially modifiable ad space that could pay for technology that would help to avoid indecent material. What drives these choices are worries about privacy. The Children's Online Privacy Protection Act (COPPA) requires parental permission for any personally identifiable information collected

---

[1] Brian Pass said that, when his company delivered large, rich-media ads—such as the movie trailer mentioned in his presentation—bandwidth costs were an issue, because the entire file was shipped all the way to the user's computer on a nightly basis. If rich-media technology starts to take hold in advertising structures, then bandwidth costs will be a factor. The myth that bandwidth is so inexpensive—that it is effectively unlimited—causes engineering decisions to be made. Milo Medin said market data show that retail pricing for Internet transport runs about $400 monthly for one megabit per second. A new entrant might get a competitive price in the range of $200. If a site draws a lot of traffic, then network providers discount substantially. For example, a Yahoo co-location facility might pay only $50, even without fiber-optic systems. If a company is willing to put content into a hosting facility that a network charges for, then the network virtually gives the bandwidth away because it provides leverage in interconnection discussions. Over the long term, the price probably will stabilize at about $150, Medin said.

about children under 13 and thus severely limits business models that would target kids.

A number of other potential privacy laws and regulations also are coming that could affect the choice of advertising-based models for online safety efforts. One is self-regulation by the industry through the Network Advertising Initiative (NAI), part of a response to the Double Click ruling. A number of industry players, including Match Logic, Double Click, 24/7 Media, and Engage, got together to find a fair way to give people notice if we want to merge personally identifiable data with ad information. The group came up with strict permission and self-regulatory standards. They worked and negotiated with the FTC to establish these standards, which were unanimously approved by the FTC and sent to the Congress and are now in force.

In discussing the data models that advertisers use and particularly the potential effect on a childrens' market, the meaning of "personally identifiable" is a huge issue. The question is how far you can move back up the chain to make data personally identifiable. According to the NAI, there will not be a move to make data nonanonymous without permission. If a hacker took the information and could match it geographically, then perhaps this could be done without permission, but it is difficult to get all the crumbs together and link them back to an actual person. Personally identifiable information usually is defined as information to be used to contact an individual directly—such as full name and physical address. E-mail address generally is defined as personally identifiable as well. Some interesting discussions are going on in the European Union about whether Internet Protocol addresses should be considered personally identifiable information. It is always difficult to figure out what will happen in the EU and which body is acting on which day.

Senators John McCain and John Kerry have proposed privacy legislation that would require Web site notice, which would affect potential children's advertisers along with everyone else, in terms of fully disclosing the facts and the privacy laws. There are also a number of other possibilities. Some in the industry favor a weakening of COPPA because of its effects in cutting off under-13s from a socially beneficial communication source. Our network does not favor a weakening of COPPA. But it has a real effect on our site. We have completely cut off under-13s from e-mail and chat, because these mechanisms can be used to spread personally identifiable information, and the costs of getting parental permission and maintaining verifiable parental permission were not justified by the revenue. Kids on our network can get to the personalization features and use them, but we keep only the first name and birth date—everything else is deleted.

On privacy, including kids' privacy, the corporate position that we have taken is that we are comfortable with further enforceable regulations saying what companies can and cannot do, as long as they are done carefully and do not forbid legitimate consumer-serving uses of data. Self-regulation, in which companies talk about their practices and expose themselves to both public scrutiny and government scrutiny for false and deceptive trade practices, will also be a major part of coming up with a privacy solution. There also will be new technology, which is the x factor. Some technologies will allow complete masking of information and covering of footsteps. This is difficult to implement. A number of advertisers will rely on the fact that people will find it difficult to use. Furthermore, not everyone wants to be anonymous at the end of the day. For instance, you want toothpaste if you run out. It is okay for most people that Webvan knows that fact because you want it to bring the toothpaste so that you do not have to leave home or worry about it. You want your refrigerator company to know when your compressor isn't operating properly so that it can come out and service it.

17

Constitutional Law and the Law of Cyberspace

Larry Lessig

17.1 INTRODUCTION

I am a professor at Stanford Law School, where I teach constitutional law and the law of cyberspace. I have been involved from the beginning in this debate about how best to solve the problem of controlling children's access to pornographic material. I got into a lot of trouble for the positions I initially took in the debate, which made me confident that I must be on to something right.

This is, necessarily, a question about the interaction between a certain technological environment and certain rules that govern that environment. This question about children's access to materials deemed harmful to minors obviously was not raised for the first time in cyberspace; it was raised many years prior in the context of real space. In real space, as Justice O'Connor said in *Reno v. ACLU*, 521 U.S. 844, 887 (1997), a majority of the states expressly regulate the rights of purveyors of pornography to sell it to children. This regulation serves an important purpose because of certain features of the architecture of real space.

It is helpful to think this through. You could suppose a community that has a law that says that if you sell pornography or other material harmful to minors, then you must assure that the person purchasing it is above the age of 18. But in addition to a law, there are clearly also norms that govern even the pornographer in his willingness to sell pornography to a child. The market, too, participates in this zoning of pornography from children; pornography costs money, and children obviously do not have a lot of money. Yet the most important thing facilitating this regulation is that, in real space, it is relatively difficult to hide the fact that you are a child. A kid might use stilts and put on a mustache and dark coat, but when the kid walks into a pornography store, the pornographer probably knows that this is a kid. In real space, age is relatively self-authenticating.

This is the single feature of the architecture of cyberspace that makes this form of regulation difficult to replicate there. Even if you have exactly the same laws, exactly the same norms, and a similar market structure, the character of the original architecture or technology of cyberspace is such that age is not relatively self-authenticating.

17.2 REGULATION IN CYBERSPACE

The question, then, is how to interact with this environment in a way that facilitates the legitimate state interest of making sure that parents have the ability to control their children's access to this stuff, while continuing to preserve the extremely important First Amendment values that exist in cyberspace. The initial reaction of civil libertarian groups was to say the government should do nothing here—that if the government did something, it would be censorship, which is banned by the First Amendment. Instead, we should allow the private market to take care of this problem.

Although the U.S. Congress passed the Communications Decency Act (CDA) of 1996, there is fairly uniform support among civil liberty organizations to strike it down for that very reason. When Bruce Ennis argued this case before the Supreme Court, he said, "Private systems, these private technologies for blocking content, will serve this function just as well as law." And the Court avers the fact that there exists private technology that could serve this purpose as well as law.

But the thing to keep in focus is that just as law regulates cyberspace, so does technology regulate cyberspace. Law and code together regulate cyberspace. Just as there is bad law so, too, there is bad code for regulating cyberspace. In my code-obsessed state of California, we say there is bad East Coast code—this is what happens in Congress—and bad West Coast code, which is what happens when people write poor technology for filtering cyberspace. The objective of someone who is worried about both free speech in cyberspace and giving parents the right type of control should be to find the mix between good East Coast and good West Coast code that gives parents this ability while preserving the maximum amount of freedom for people who should not be affected by this type of regulation.

In my view, when the civil liberties organizations said government should do nothing, they were wrong. They were wrong because it created a huge market for the development of bad West Coast code—blocking software, or censor-ware, which made it possible for companies to filter out content on the Web. The reason I call this type of technology "bad code" is that it filters much too broadly relative to the legitimate state interest in facilitating the control of parents over their children's access to materials that are harmful to them.

There is a lot of good evidence about how poorly this technology filters cyberspace: how it filters the wrong type of material. There are also more insidious examples of what the companies that release this software do. For example, if you become known as a critic of that software, mysteriously your Web site may appear on the list of blocked Web sites, which becomes an extraordinary blacklist of banned books. The problem with this blacklist of banned books is that the public cannot look at it. It is a secret list—a secret list of filtered sites that is being sold to the public on account of parents' legitimate desire to find a way to protect their children.

17.3 POSSIBLE SOLUTIONS

My view is that there is a mixture of government and market actions that could help facilitate the type of control that parents deserve while minimizing the bad effects of this West Coast code. I will describe two versions of it. One is more problematic; the other is more invasive.

Imagine a browser that allows you to select G-rated surfing. As the browser perused the Web, the client would signal to the server that this person wants G-rated browsing. This means that, if you have material that is harmful to minors on your site, you cannot serve that G-rated browser this material. The necessary law to make the regime work is simply a requirement that sites respect the request that only G-rated material be sent to a particular client. All that is required is that you forbid people from sending so-called "harmful-to-minors" material to a browser that says, "I want G-rated material."

If there were such a law—and only that law—then there would be a strong incentive for the market to develop many browser technologies that would signal efficiently, "I want G-rated material." A family in a particular house could have many different accounts on the browser, so that children have G-rated accounts and the parents do not. The market would provide the technology to make that system work.

One problem with this system is that, by going around and raising your hand and saying, "I want G-rated browsing material," you are also saying, "I am likely to be a child." People who want to abuse children can then take advantage of that hand-waving in ways that we obviously do not want. There is a way around this problem, but let us move to the second solution, which I think solves it more directly.

Imagine a law that says, "You must, if you have a Web site, have a certain tag at the server or the page level that signals the presence of material that is harmful to minors." This is the type of judgment that bookstores have to make now. It is not an easy judgment, but it is one already entrusted to booksellers today. An incentive is thereby created in the market for the development of a G-rated browser, but this time it does not signal its use by a child. It simply looks for this particular tag. If it finds this tag, then it does not give the user access to the Web site.

This, too, is a mixture of a certain amount of regulation, which says "you must tag this content," and a certain expectation about how the market will respond. To the extent that parents want to protect their children, they will adopt versions of the browser that facilitate this blocking on the basis of age. To the extent they do not want to protect their children, they will not use these types of browsers. But the power either to adopt the technology to block access or not will be within the hands of parents. Obviously, browsers—at least in the current browser war—are inexpensive; Microsoft has promised they will be free forever. Thus, the cost of the technology implemented from the parents' side is very low.

The advantage to this approach is that the only people blocked by this system are either parents who opt to use the blocking or schools that adopt browsers that facilitate blocking to protect children from harmful content while at school. It does not have the over-inclusiveness problem that the other solutions tend to have. Because the incentive is structured so that all we need to worry about is material harmful to minors, it does not create an incentive to block much more broadly than what the law legitimately can require.[1]

If Geoff Stone[2] were here, he would say, "Yes, but aren't you forcing Web sites to speak, by forcing them to put these little tags on their systems? And so isn't this a compelled speech, and isn't that a violation of the Constitution?" I think the answer is no, because the relevant compelled speech is not that you must display on your Web site a banner that

---

[1] Milo Medin said he likes this scheme because there are many ways of implementing it— not only in a browser, but also as a service that a user could buy from a network provider. The provider would be able to look at the tags as part of the caching process, and people would not be subject to the usual workarounds on the software side. Another appealing aspect is that it puts all the people who want to cooperate on one side of the issue. The other people do not want to cooperate and do not want their stuff to be restricted. The question is, what incentives do these people have? Many personal publishers, who publish just because it is fun, would be affected directly by this. It would not affect the large companies, because they would act rationally.

[2] Geoff Stone, from the University of Chicago, spoke on the First Amendment at the committee's first meeting, in July 2000.

says, "This is material harmful to minors." It is not that you must, in any public way, advertise this characteristic. You simply enable the Web site to label itself properly through the HTML code in the background. The Supreme Court has upheld the right of states to force providers of material harmful to minors to discriminate in the distribution of this material. It seems to me perfectly consistent with that opinion to say that sites that have this type of material must put a hidden tag in it that facilitates the type of blocking that would enable parents to regain some kind of control.

Geoff Stone taught me the First Amendment, so I understand his perspective toward it. But I think he is undercounting how this action looks in light of the other things Congress has done. There is a certain pragmatic character to how the Supreme Court decides cases; the court will not say the Congress can never do anything until the end of time. This type of regulation seems to me to be a relatively slight intrusion that would facilitate a better free-speech environment than would exist in the absence of any federal regulation. If we had no federal regulation at all, the result would be, for example, the blocking of many sites about contraception using private filters. In this way, the First Amendment world is worse without this regulation than with it.

The necessary condition for success is not an agreement about what material is harmful to minors but rather what the language of the harmful-to-minor tag would be. The former would be left to the ordinary system of letting people decide what the character of the material is and self-rating. The standard imposed by the Supreme Court is that you must adopt the least-restrictive means. CDA-1 failed because it was overly broad in trying to regulate things that were clearly not speech harmful to minors and because it created too much of a burden on users by requiring them to carry IDs around if they wanted to use the Web. I think CDA-2 will be struck down because it continues to require that you carry an ID. These burdens would have to be borne by everyone who wanted to use the Web, just so that children could be protected.

In my scenario, the burden is borne by Web site administrators, who already are spending extraordinary amounts of money developing their Web pages. It is just one more tag. No one can argue that the marginal cost of one more tag is expensive. What is expensive is making a judgment about your Web site. But if you are in the pornography business, then it is an easy judgment. If you are in the business of advising children about access to contraception, then I think it is an easy judgment. The Starr report[3] is not harmful to minors. There would be difficult cases, but the law passed by Congress requires these difficult decisions anyway.

---

[3]This is a reference to the 1998 report by Independent Counsel Kenneth Starr on President Clinton's relationship with a White House intern.

I envision the G-rating feature as an opt-in setting on a browser. It could be a default instead,[4] but I contend that if parents do not know how to turn on the G-rating feature, then they ought to learn. Constitutionally, opting out clearly is different from opting in. The way to analyze the constitutional balancing test is as follows: is the additional burden placed on the 100 million people who do not have children and do not care about protecting children worth the advantage of making sure that the 60 million people who do want to protect children do not have to take any extra steps? I cannot predict how this type of judgment would be made. But as the market develops, people will start branding themselves, much like AOL has done. One reason why AOL likes the existing system so much is that the company draws a lot of parents to its content, because it has taken many steps to provide for them.

Age verification would be performed by the family in switching the browser on or off the G-rating setting. This is the big difference between this type of a solution and the CDA type of solution, in which age verification is done over the Internet. With age verification over the Internet, the incentives for cheating are big, so the system needs to be sophisticated enough to prevent it.

My proposal suggests a two-tier system in a library setting,[5] with one tier available to children and either available to adults. Just as libraries now might have an adult section that is not accessible to children, you can imagine having some browsers that are G-rated and others that are not. It is difficult to know the library's role in enforcing the rule on children, however. Some libraries have adopted the practice of requiring a child's library card to be marked. I am less concerned about libraries enforcing this rule when only a tiny fraction of speech is being regulated, as opposed to many types of speech. It does suggest some minimal role for librarians.[6]

---

[4]Linda Hodge noted that most parents are not using filters and suggested that the G-rating feature be a default, requiring action to opt out. To disable the G-rating feature, a user could change the default setting. Milo Medin said the ISPs supply browsers and provide an option either at startup or in an upgrade panel that asks the user to "check this or that."

[5]Marilyn Mason said that one of the most troublesome things about the current legislation is that it puts the burden of deciding what is harmful to minors on the shoulders of every school and library. She said aspects of Lessig's proposal are appealing: the least-restrictive setting becomes the norm, the list of what is G-rated or not is public, a challenge is a public event, public agencies are removed from the middle, and millions of people are relieved of the burden of deciding what "harmful to minors" means.

[6]Marilyn Mason said the tier system could be handled with a library card or smart card. An adult has an adult card so there is no problem. Children have their parents sign for their cards. If a parent wants a child to have unlimited access, then the card can be so coded. The cards can be read by machine. David Forsyth said librarians have told the committee that

There are problems with the system I have described, but only with those involving a state regulation that attempts to guarantee that material harmful to minors is not handed over to children without the permission of parents. My concept is more complicated because it involves the Internet, but it anticipates the same type of problem that exists in the majority of states now, when material like this is distributed.

Sites would have to do self-rating. Importantly, the self-rating would not go beyond this category of harmful to minors. PICS technology, the Platform for Internet Content Selection, enables site rating in a wide range of circumstances. PICS is the same technology as P3P, the Platform for Privacy Preferences Project, but is applied to material harmful to minors. (I am skeptical of PICS because it enables general labeling, which is much broader than the legitimate interest at issue when dealing with material harmful to minors. Its architecture is such that the label or filter can be imposed anywhere in the distribution chain. If the world turned out the way the PICS author wanted, you would have many rich filtering systems that could become the tools of censors who wanted to prevent access to speech about China or the like. My proposal involves a much narrower label.)

To avoid asking a site to slander itself, the label could be an equivalent to the one on cigarette packets. This label does not say, "I think this is harmful to your health." It says only that the Surgeon General thinks cigarettes are harmful to your health. An equivalent entity could find material harmful to minors. The label would not actually say this—it would be a computer code, of course. On the other hand, I could reveal the code and see it, so you might say that this is equivalent to self-slander, although I am not sure where the harm is. The label means that the speech is of a class that can be restricted. We could make up a word and call it "XYZ speech." I can be required to block children's access to XYZ speech. The law cannot force me to keep the speech away from my own children. All this does is improve the vocabulary of the space so that people can make decisions in a relatively consistent frame.

---

they already monitor library activity and discourage users who are making others uncomfortable or behaving inappropriately. It might not be necessary for a library to require children to identify themselves before using the Internet; the "tap on the shoulder" mechanism probably can deal with it. Milo Medin said this approach moves the incentive for labeling or doing the labor to the content publishers, as opposed to the people who do not want to be affected. This localizes the problem and trims a wide range of responsibility. Labeling provides the negative incentive needed for the system to work.

We cannot simply create a dot-xxx space for material harmful to minors because there are other types of potentially harmful speech besides hardcore pornography. Here Geoff Stone would appear in full force, and I am behind him now. The fact that you force me to go into a dot-xxx space is harmful to me if I do not convey hardcore pornography but rather other material that perhaps should not be given to children. You are forcing me to associate with a space that has a certain kind of meaning. If that were the only option, then maybe it would be constitutionally acceptable. But there is no reason to force me to associate with the hardcore pornographers when an invisible filtering/zoning system, such as the P3P labels in the HTML tag, can be employed instead. I can be a dot-com and be tagged. Some of my Web pages would be blocked to a child, whereas others would not. Because I have both types of content, I contend that I should be free to be a dot-org or dot-com and not be forced into the dot-xxx ghetto.

Of course, a site might take the position that the First Amendment protects it in delivering my material to children, regardless of what the parents think. The parents might have a different view, thinking they should be allowed to block access to that site. The point about this structure is that the question would be resolved in a public context. If the parents believe that this material properly is considered harmful to minors, and the site refuses to label it as such, then there would be an adjudication of whether this is material harmful to minors. I am much happier to have this adjudication in the context of a First Amendment tradition, which does limit the degree to which you can restrict speech, as opposed to a cyberspace board meeting, where the real issue is, "How is this going to play in the market if people think we're accepting this kind of speech?" In my view, we can ensure more protection of free speech if we have that argument in the context of adjudicators, who understand the tradition of free speech that we are trying to protect.

I want to emphasize that it would be stupid and probably unconstitutional to make the requirement to label punishable through a criminal sanction. We want to keep the punishment low in order to preserve this proposed system against constitutional challenge. To the extent that you raise the punishment, the Supreme Court is likely to say, "This is too dangerous, and it will chill speech if you threaten 30 years in jail because someone failed to properly tag a site." Alternatively, I like causes of action. I push this in the context of spam all the time. A cause of action might be one in which bounty hunters were deployed to find sites that they believe are harmful to minors. They would then employ some system for adjudicating this issue. Then you would get lots of efficient enforcement technology out there, for people who really care about this issue, and the enforcement would be enforced in a context in which the

First Amendment is the constraint as opposed to a corporate context in which the board worries about public relations.

You have to implement this solution step by step. You have to be open to the fact that we do not understand well enough how the different factors interact. We can make speculations, but we need to use real data to analyze it, and this requires some experience in taking one step and evaluating it. The Web is the first place to worry about. You could play with that for a year or more and see what works, and then decide where else you need to deploy this solution. Usenet is a network that uses an NTP protocol. An ISP can decide which protocols to allow across its network. It might say, I am a G-rated ISP and will not allow any Usenet services to come across. Sometimes people get access to the Usenet through the Web. In these cases, you can still require the same kind of filtering. It is only in the context of getting access to Usenet outside of the Web that a problem arises.[7]

17.4 PRACTICAL CONSIDERATIONS

Let me map out a sample proceeding. Let us say there has been a failure to properly tag something that is, in fact, harmful to minors. Imagine that something like a bounty is available. The bounty hunter brings an action: hopefully not a federal court action. In principle, anyone could bring the action. The person says, "This site by Playboy has material that is properly considered harmful to minors, and they have not implemented this tag." Then there has to be a judgment about whether the material is, in fact, harmful to minors. A court must make this type of judgment, as they always have done. It is difficult in some cases, but the public has long survived this judgment being made in real space. If the court finds that this is material harmful to minors and the site has not put up this tag, then there would be some sanction. I think the sanction should be a civil sanction, such as a fine, sufficient to achieve compliance, that is, set at a

---

[7]Dick Thornburgh said the person doing the conversion from Usenet to the Web would end up doing the labeling, not the person who posts the content. In this example, the problem is not difficult to solve. But the generic issue is that there is some level of restriction on the connection; it is not necessarily a complete removal of either an intermediary or software on the PC, although it greatly facilitates things. There is no reason why you could not enforce the same type of labeling requirement on the publisher. There is usually a way of labeling files available via file transfer protocol or other types of protocols, for example. It could apply to chat groups, instant messaging traffic, and so on. The key point is to shift the burden, make it general enough that people have an incentive to cooperate, and enable bounty hunters so the marketplace can police it and you would not necessarily need law enforcement.

level such that a rational businessperson thinks, "It's cheaper for us to comply."

You could assume that no one would comply with this law, that there would be thousands of these prosecutions, and it would bog down the courts and end up like the war on drugs. This situation would be similar to a denial-of-service attack[8] and would prove that this system is terrible. On the other hand, you could assume that people will behave rationally based on what they expect the consequences and cost of compliance will be. Then the world segregates into a vast majority that are willing to comply because it is cheaper and they do not wish to violate the law anyway and a smaller number that we have to worry about controlling.

A bounty action could be structured so that the first to file gets to litigate, and, after a judgment is rendered, that is the end of it. If a frivolous action is filed, it should be punishable by a filing for malicious prosecution. A class action analogy is possible, but the cumbersome nature of class actions now might make it simpler to have just a single action. I do not think it is possible to eliminate the possibility of a proliferation of actions, but there are ways to try. For instance, we could limit it by geographic district, for example, to avoid the problem of trying to sue someone across the country and imposing that type of burden. A lot of creative thinking will be needed. A qui tam action[9] could be troubling constitutionally. There are people who believe that a party should be found to lack standing unless there is a demonstration of harm.[10] But there is such a long tradition of qui tam that, like bounty actions, it will survive.

The one area of this jurisprudence that has not been developed is whether and how the community standards component of the traditional obscenity doctrine applies in the context of material harmful to minors. There is a need for the courts to figure out something new. The decision in the Third Circuit, *ACLU v. Reno,* 217 F.3d 162 (3rd Cir. 2000), striking

---

[8]David Forsyth sought to draw an analogy to a denial-of-service attack in which a large number of people do a small inappropriate thing on a network and overload the system administrator. In the legal context, a sufficient number of small bounty-seeking actions from enough different people would bring the system to a halt.

[9]A qui tam action is one filed in court by a private individual who sees some misconduct that is actionable under the law. If the individual prevails in court, he or she is entitled to some of the proceeds that the transgressor must pay.

[10]David Forsyth questioned whether bounty hunters could participate in civil actions, because he thought that some harm had to be demonstrated in order to sue. Dick Thornburgh said that, in a qui tam case, the evidence brought forth as the basis of the action must be something peculiar to the individual. A person cannot walk in off the street and bring a qui tam claim by showing a simple fact such as a lack of a tag on a program. These claims are numerous within an industry where evidence has been accumulated and there is only one person or a small group of people who could bring an action.

down the most recent action of Congress made it sound as if there is no possible way to get over the community standards problem when trying to regulate this material in cyberspace, because there are so many different communities and problems associated with applying different types of tests. What if the architecture requires you to label or unlabel depending on where, geographically, a person is coming from? The way the architecture is now, it is relatively difficult to figure out where a user is located. This is where the additional layer of community standards becomes difficult to architect. I confess that I do not know how to solve this problem.

The Supreme Court is difficult to predict. My confidence in predicting what this Court will do has dropped dramatically in the last year, so I will not predict how the Court will resolve this issue. But I cannot believe that it will decide that nothing can be done. The resolution will not be that one standard fits the whole nation either; the Court will instead attempt to find some compromise. In a sense, it has struck the same balance in real space through the same legal standard applied to real-space materials.

This leads to the question of how the community standards issue would play out in a place like a library, which serves a wide range of people, presumably with different ideas of what is harmful. If there were thousands of lawsuits, this could create a chilling effect on free speech, because people would think, "Well, every time I have a certain type of speech on my site, I'm going to get into a lawsuit. It will be blocked, so I'm not going to have that speech on this site (without labeling)." Yet we often forget that, with the existing censorware, Web sites already make the same judgment. They say, "Hmm. I want to avoid getting on the CYBERSitter list. I want to include this interesting information about how to get contraception in certain cases, but it's too dangerous, because this speech will be filtered. When my speech is filtered in the context of CYBERSitter, there is no court to which I can go to order that it is improper to filter my speech. I am stuck."

In other words, there is already a chilling effect on free speech created by these invisible blacklists that spread across cyberspace. I do not think we can avoid some chilling effect. The question is how to minimize it. Focusing on a legal standard that is interpreted in a legal context is a way to minimize the chilling effect and maximize the amount of speech that can be protected.

"Chill" has a more precise meaning than just causing you to not post material. It means that you are uncertain and afraid of punishment, so you choose not to post what otherwise you should be allowed to post. It is the variance (the uncertainty in application) that we are concerned about. Given the range of private censors, the variance that we need to consider is much greater than it would be if there were a single standard defining material harmful to minors. Thus, I think that "chill" has greater meaning in the private censorship context than in the government context. This is not to say that we could not imagine the court developing a doctrine such that people are terrified and do not do anything. That is an unavoidable consequence if you screw it up and would be terrible for free speech. Maybe this is a lawyer-centric view, but I am much happier if that battle occurs in court, because then I have the right to argue that this standard is wrong and inconsistent. When it is done in the private censorship context, I do not have the right to make that argument.

Here is the disingenuous part of my scenario. It is extremely difficult to say what the standard "harmful to minors" means. The burden is on the government or prosecutor to demonstrate that this material is harmful to minors. I have the right to free speech until the state can demonstrate this. But what does the government actually have to show? The government does not need to show data that demonstrate the harm. The way these cases are typically litigated involves comparisons to "like kinds" of material. Obscenity is harmful to minors. As the court said, the sort of sexually explicit speech that appropriately is kept from children is like obscenity to children.

To date, "harmful to minors" has been interpreted by the Supreme Court to include sexually explicit speech only. It does not include hate speech, for example. There is a lower court judgment that expands the interpretation, but I don't believe that interpretation will be sustained. Therefore, in my view, the legitimate interest of the government has been prescribed to include only sexually explicit speech. I am sure that people will try to bring other types of speech to the courts. But I am also sure that the Supreme Court would look at Ku Klux Klan (KKK) speech, for example, and say, "It is terrible speech, I agree, but this is the core of First Amendment type of speech that we must protect." We will get into an argument about whether 6-year-olds should see KKK speech, and this will be difficult for the court.

I have no kids and I do not look at this material. I have no way of figuring out how to draw the line. But part of the solution is to realize that no one will have a complete solution. We depend on the diversity of institutions to contribute their parts. Some part has to be contributed by people making judgments. In a paper that I wrote with Paul Resnick, who was originally on this committee, we described techniques for minimizing the cost of determining what "harmful to minors" means. Geoff Stone would look at some of these techniques and say, "No, no, the Constitution would forbid them."

Imagine a site asking a government agency, "Can you give me a sign that this material is okay?" This is like a promise not to prosecute, and it is done now. It amounts to preclearance of material that is on the borderline. It is not saying that you cannot publish unless you get permission. It is not saying that if you do not get permission, you cannot publish. All it means is that if you get preclearance, there is a guarantee that you will not be punished. It is a safe harbor—it takes care of the "chill" problem. If the government says, "We can't give you a safe harbor here," then you have a problem. Then you must decide whether it is worth the risk to speak. But, again, this is a problem we face now. People currently make this decision when they decide how to distribute material in more than half of the states. We should minimize the cost of that problem, but I do not think we can say the Constitution requires us to make that cost zero.

As times and standards change, crude standards help, because a fine-grained system would become out-of-date.[11] Because this discriminator is so crude, I think that what happens in cyberspace would mirror what would happen in real space—people only worry about and prosecute the extreme cases. There is a lot of material floating around that nobody wastes time worrying about. But, in principle, we would have to worry about how things are updated over time. In cyberspace, 10 years is a long time. I am not sure what the burden of that is. My personal preference is that we do as little as possible but enough to avoid the problem of too much private censorship. The system also needs to be sensitive to what we learn about the consequences of what we do.

This solution will not eliminate all private filtering. But my view is that a significant amount of demand for private filtering results from the lack of any less-restrictive alternative. If you asked the filtering companies, 90 percent of them would say, "What Lessig is talking about is terrible and unconstitutional"—because it would drive 90 percent of them out of business. But there still would be parents who are on the Christian Right, for example, and who want to add another layer of protection on top. We will not go from a world of perfect censorship to perfect free speech, but a balance is needed between the two. Under the existing system, we have so many examples of overreaching and private censoring that some way to undermine it is needed.

Given the international context for the Internet, this solution is not a

---

[11]Bob Schloss asked who would label orphan content, which is floating around on the Internet or on hard disks but whose publisher is dead or not paying attention, and how the binary indicator—a yes or no answer to the question of whether something is harmful to minors—would hold up over time as community standards changed. It might work for 10 years, but in the end, to deal with the problem of both shifting standards and orphan content, the system could end up with a third-party rating process again.

complete one. But our nation is very powerful. When you set up a simple system for people to comply with, and there is some threat that they will be attacked by the United States if they are not in compliance, then it will be easier for most people to comply. Tiny sanctions and tiny compliance costs actually have a significant effect on convincing people to obey.

Appendix:

Biographies of Presenters

Nicholas Belkin has been professor of information science in the School of Communication, Information, and Library Studies at Rutgers University since 1985. Prior to that appointment, he was lecturer and then senior lecturer in the Department of Information Science at the City University, London, from 1975. He has held visiting positions at the University of Western Ontario, the Free University of Berlin, and the Integrated Publication and Information Systems Institute of the German National Research Center for Computer Science and was visiting scientist at the Institute of Systems Science of the National University of Singapore and a Fulbright Fellow at the Department of Information Studies, University of Tampere, Finland. Professor Belkin was chair of the ACM Special Interest Group on Information Retrieval from 1995 to 1999 and is a member of the Steering Committee for the ACM/IEEE Joint Conferences on Digital Libraries. He received his Ph.D. in information studies from the University of London in 1977 and a master's in librarianship from the University of Washington in 1970.

Michel Bilello holds a Ph.D. degree in electrical engineering and an M.D. degree, both from Stanford University. His most recent research includes security mediation for secure dissemination of medical information. He has recently completed his internship in internal medicine.

Fred Cotton is director of training services for SEARCH, the National Consortium for Justice Information and Statistics. He provides technical assistance and training to local, state, and federal criminal justice agencies nationwide in information systems, including assistance in computer crimes investigations and examining seized microcomputers. He instructs a variety of technology crimes courses that SEARCH offers at its National Criminal Justice Computer Laboratory and Training Center in Sacramento, California, and at other sites nationwide, and he oversees a training staff of eight. He has also taught advanced officer courses and officer safety subjects in the Basic Police Academy and was an invited guest of Norway's National Bureau of Criminal Investigation, where he provided training on computer investigations. Mr. Cotton has 13 years of full-time law enforcement service as a field supervisor with experience in operations, investigations, records, training, and data processing. In addition to his duties at SEARCH, he is a reserve police officer with the Yuba City, California, Police Department, where he is assigned to the Sacramento Valley High-Tech Crimes Task Force, and a specialist reserve officer with the Los Angeles Police Department, where he is assigned to the Organized Crime and Vice Division. Mr. Cotton is a member of the Florida Computer Crime Investigators Association, the Forensic Association of Computer Technicians, the Northern California Chapter of the High Technology Crime Investigation Association (HTCIA), the National Technical Investigators Association, the Georgia High-Tech Crime Consortium, the Midwestern Electronic Crime Investigation Association, the American Society of Law Enforcement Trainers, and Police Futurist International. He is a former member of the National Board of Directors of HTCIA. In September 1999, the International Board of Directors of HTCIA selected him as the first recipient of its Distinguished Achievement Award. Mr. Cotton is certified by the California Commission on Peace Officer Standards and Training as a "computer / white-collar crime investigator" for the State of California through the Robert J. Presley Institute of Criminal Investigation (ICI), and he is an ICI-certified instructor. He is also a graduate of and has been a guest instructor at the "Seized Computer Evidence Recovery Specialist" training course offered through the Federal Law Enforcement Training Center in Glynco, Georgia, and he has qualified and testified as an expert witness on computer investigations in both county and federal courts. Mr. Cotton holds a degree in administration of justice and is an adjunct professor in the forensic computer investigation certificate program of the University of New Haven, Connecticut.

Donald Eastlake has over 30 years of experience in the computer field and was one of the principal architects and specification authors for the Domain Name System security protocol. He co-chairs the joint IETF/W3C XML Digital Signature Working Group, chairs the e-commerce-oriented IETF TRADE Working Group, is a member of and co-editor of the specification for the W3C XML Encryption Working Group, and a member of the Java Community group developing XML Security APIs. He is a member of the technical staff at Motorola and has previously worked for IBM, CyberCash, Digital Equipment Corporation, Transfinite Systems Company, Computer Corporation of America, and the Massachusetts Institute of Technology.

Susan Getgood is one of corporate America's leading experts on education and Internet safety. She has testified on behalf of the industry before Congress, the National Research Council, the Federal Trade Commission, and the Children's Online Protection Act Commission. Prior to assuming her current role, she served as the Learning Company's director of corporate communications, where she developed a broad knowledge of the role of technology in teaching both children and adults. She previously was director of marketing at Microsystems Software, the company that developed Cyber Patrol Internet filtering software. She represented Microsystems Software when it was among the coalition of plaintiffs who successfully challenged the constitutionality of the Communications Decency Act in 1996. In December 1997, she was part of a panel on Internet filtering and other technologies to protect children at the White House-backed "Internet/Online Summit: Focus on Kids." She has been involved in issues related to creating positive digital content for children and the development of quality educational content for homes and schools. She is on the Board of Directors of Mass Networks and was recently named to the Executive Committee of this public-private partnership dedicated to enhancing education through technology in the state of Massachusetts.

Bennett Haselton has been publishing reports on the workings of Internet blocking software since 1996. His Web site at Peacefire.org has functioned as a clearinghouse of information related to Internet blocking software and has been featured in reports on CNN, CourtTV, CNNfn, MTV News, and MSNBC. Bennett holds an M.A. in mathematics from Vanderbilt University and lives in Seattle. He currently works as a "contract hacker," finding security holes in Internet applications on a commission basis.

Chris Kelly has served in a variety of business, educational, and governmental roles over the past 10 years aimed at bettering the ways we provide customer service, teach our children, and live our everyday lives online. Currently chief privacy officer for Excite@Home, the leading broadband online service provider, he is responsible for the company's privacy policy and practices, working with public policy makers and industry leaders on consumer privacy initiatives and educating the public regarding the company's commitment to online privacy. He brings extensive experience in information technology, law, and public policy to his role at Excite@Home. At Kendara, a 40-person next-generation digital marketing startup acquired by Excite@Home in 2000, he served as one of the online industry's first chief privacy officers, overseeing product architecture development and data management practices to ensure consumer privacy. Prior to Kendara, he was an attorney in the Antitrust and Intellectual Property groups at Palo Alto law firm Wilson, Sonsini, Goodrich & Rosati, where he counseled numerous Internet companies on privacy policies, terms of service, and other Web site service concerns. At Wilson Sonsini, he also advised numerous Silicon Valley companies on the implications of the government's antitrust suit against Microsoft and on the application of intellectual property concepts in the digital age. As a fellow of the Berkman Center for Internet and Society at Harvard Law School, he worked on a variety of Internet public policy issues, including spam prevention, privacy protection, and technology's impact on education. He has also taught cyberspace law as an adjunct professor at the California Western School of Law in San Diego. In the community, he serves on the board of directors of Greatschools.net, a not-for-profit online "Zagat's Guide" to every school in California and Arizona, assisting the company's nationwide expansion efforts. He also participates in the Palo Alto Area Bar Association's Lawyers in the Schools program, teaching high school students basic legal concepts through interactive role playing exercises. He is a member of the State Bar of California and the American Bar Association. He has served as a policy analyst for the White House Domestic Policy Council and as a special assistant at the U.S. Department of Education. He holds a J.D. from Harvard Law School, a master's degree in political science from Yale University, and a B.A. from Georgetown University, where he was elected to Phi Beta Kappa. At Harvard, he was editor in chief of the *Harvard Journal of Law and Technology* and was part of the founding team for the Berkman Center for Internet & Society.

Ray Larson specializes in the design and performance evaluation of information retrieval systems and the evaluation of user interaction with those systems. His background includes work as a programmer/analyst with the University of California (UC) Division of Library Automation, where he was involved in the design, development, and performance evaluation of the UC public access online union catalog (MELVYL). His research has concentrated on the design and evaluation of information retrieval systems. He is the designer of the Cheshire II information retrieval system, which is being used as a search engine at numerous sites in the United States and Europe. The ranking algorithms developed in the Cheshire II project are the basis of the Inktomi search engine used by Yahoo and other World Wide Web search portals. He was a faculty investigator on the Sequoia 2000 project, where he was involved in the design and evaluation of a very-large-scale, network-based information system to support the information needs of scientists studying global change. He is also a faculty investigator on the UC Berkeley Environmental Digital Library Project (sponsored by the National Science Foundation (NSF), the National Aeronautics and Space Administration, and the Defense Advanced Research Projects Agency (DARPA)), where the work is continuing on a very large environmental information system providing access to information on the California environment. He is the principal investigator on the International Digital Libraries Initiative sponsored by NSF and the Joint Information Systems Committee in the United Kingdom. He is a co-principal investigator on other projects sponsored by DARPA and the Institute for Museum and Library Studies. He has consulted on information retrieval systems and automatic classification methods with major corporations, including Sun Microsystems, American Express, and Inktomi. He has also consulted on international information system projects in the United States and the United Kingdom, including the Networked Social Science Tools and Resources project and the "Archives Hub" linking archival collections in U.K. research libraries.

David Lewis is a consultant based in Chicago, Illinois. He works in the areas of information retrieval, machine learning, and natural language processing. Prior to taking up consulting, he was a researcher at AT&T Labs and Bell Labs and a research faculty member at the University of Chicago. Lewis received his Ph.D. in computer science from the University of Massachusetts at Amherst in 1992 and has undergraduate degrees in computer science and mathematics from Michigan State University. He has published more than 40 papers, holds 5 patents, and helped to design the U.S. Government Message Understanding Conference and Text Retrieval Conference evaluations of language processing technology.

David Maher has served as chief technology officer of InterTrust since July 1999. Before joining InterTrust, he was an AT&T fellow, division manager, and head of the Secure Systems Research Department at AT&T Labs, where he was working on secure IP networks and secure electronic commerce protocols. He joined Bell Labs in 1981, where he developed secure wideband transmission systems, cryptographic key management systems, and secure communications devices. He was chief architect for AT&T's STU-III secure voice, data, and video products used by the White House and U.S. intelligence and military personnel for top secret communications. In 1992 Maher was made a Bell Labs fellow in recognition of his work on communications security. He was also chief scientist for AT&T Secure Communications Systems overseeing secure systems R&D at Bell Labs, Gretag Data systems in Zurich, and Datotek Systems in Dallas. In 1993, Maher designed the Information Vending Encryption System used to provide a "virtual VCR" video pay-per-view system for cable networks.

In 1995, he worked with AT&T Universal Card Services, where he designed and analyzed a number of electronic payment systems and served as a member of the Mondex International Security Group. He has published papers in the fields of combinatorics, cryptography, number theory, signal processing, and electronic commerce. He has been a consultant to the National Science Foundation, National Security Agency, National Institute of Standards and Technology, and the Congressional Office of Technology Assessment. He has a Ph.D. in mathematics from Lehigh University, and he has taught electrical engineering, mathematics, and computer science at several institutions and was an associate professor of mathematics at Worcester Polytechnic Institute. He currently serves on the Computer Science and Telecommunications Board committee investigating networked systems of embedded computers.

Deirdre Mulligan is acting clinical professor of law and director of the Samuelson Law, Technology, and Public Policy Clinic at the Boalt Hall School of Law, University of California at Berkeley. Prior to joining Boalt, she was staff counsel at the Center for Democracy and Technology, where she focused on privacy and First Amendment issues. She serves on the Computer Science and Telecommunications Board committee studying authentication techniques and their implications for privacy.

Brian Pass is a partner with the law firm of Brown, Raysman, Millstein, Felder, and Steiner LLP, heading the firm's West Coast technology practice from its Los Angeles office. Mr. Pass represents clients in the licensing, development, and distribution of computer software; hardware development and OEM relationships; new media and Web site licensing, development, and marketing; intellectual property and trade secret protection; broadband communications; interactive television; and e-commerce. Mr. Pass counsels companies on start-up formation and venture capital finance, joint venture formation, and mergers and acquisitions. He also advises companies on Internet privacy and other regulatory issues affecting new media and e-commerce. Before joining Brown Raysman, he served as president, chief executive officer, and co-founder of Passport New Media, where he led the development of Passport's critically acclaimed children's Internet service, Your Own World. At Passport, he raised $7.5 million in venture capital and led a team of over 30 employees, while concluding numerous third-party content partnerships and negotiating key technology and distribution relationships. He also served as vice president and general counsel at Americast, a joint venture of the Walt Disney Corporation and several of the Baby Bell telephone companies, to develop interactive digital television systems. In addition to advising the Americast partnership and its board on all general corporate matters, he negotiated and administered numerous technology purchasing and licensing agreements, including a $1 billion set-top box purchase agreement; an $80 million dollar hardware purchase agreement; a multimillion dollar intellectual property licensing agreement; and numerous software development and licensing agreements. He graduated from Wesleyan University in 1986 with high honors in the College of Social Studies and received his J.D. from the UCLA School of Law in 1991.

Hinrich Schütze is chief technical officer and co-founder of Novation Biosciences, a data and text mining company serving the pharmaceutical industry. He was formerly co-founder and Vice president of advanced development for Outride, Inc., where he applied state-of-the-art relevance technology to the challenge of information retrieval.

Eddie Zeitler was a senior vice president at Charles Schwab & Co., Inc., through March 2001, where for 5 years he managed the Information Security Department, which comprised six specialized units: Information Access and Protection, Information Security Technology, Information Security Risk Management, Information Security Strategy and Architecture, Business Contingency Planning, and Security Awareness and Training. Mr. Zeitler has a varied background in computers and information processing. Prior to Charles Schwab, he managed the information security functions at Fidelity Investments, Bank of America, and Security Pacific National Bank. Other management positions include the capacity planning function for Security Pacific National Bank's computer centers, technical services (operating systems and software) and computer center operations for the National Data Center of Federated Department Stores, and data center performance and configuration for Transamerica Information Services. He began his career developing the operating system used on the Shuttle Orbiter at Rockwell International and radar system controls at ITT Gilfillan. External activities include participation on various committees such as the Los Angeles County Computer Crime Task Force, the Department of the Treasury's Financial Management Services Security Advisory Panel, the ANSI X9.E9 and X9.F2 Working Groups for Security of Financial Systems, the U.S. Treasury's Electronic Funds Transfer Task Force Subcommittee on Interoperability, the ABA Information Systems Security Committee, the (ISC)2 Qualifications Review Committee, the National Computer System Security and Privacy Advisory Board, and the National Research Council's Panel for Information Technology that annually reviews the National Institute of Standards and Technology's information technology program. Mr. Zeitler is a registered brokerage representative (Series 7 and Series 63) and is a certified information systems security professional. He holds a B.S. in mathematics and an M.S. in systems engineering from the University of Arizona. He also completed his Ph.D. candidacy in computer science at the University of Alberta.